NEW TESTAMENT GUIDES

General Editor
A.T. Lincoln

THE JOHANNINE EPISTLES

THE JOHANNINE EPISTLES

Ruth B. Edwards

Sheffield Academic Press

Copyright © 1996 Sheffield Academic Press

Published by Sheffield Academic Press Ltd
Mansion House
19 Kingfield Road
Sheffield S11 9AS
England

Printed on acid-free paper in Great Britain
by The Cromwell Press
Melksham, Wiltshire

British Library Cataloguing in Publication Data

A catalogue record for this book is available
from the British Library

ISBN 1-85075-750-X

Contents

Acknowledgments

It is a pleasure to thank all who have contributed to the writing of this book, especially the series editor, Dr Andrew Lincoln, both for the initial invitation and his helpful comments on my draft, the staff of Queen Mother Library, University of Aberdeen, for their courteous assistance and perseverance in obtaining inter-library loans, and my husband Patrick for his patience and unfailing support. Above all, I should like to thank colleagues, friends and students, past and present, in the Department of Divinity with Religious Studies and the former Department of Classics for their interest and encouragement, and the stimulus they have given me to engage in Johannine studies. This book is dedicated to them in gratitude for the community we have shared over more then thirty years

Aberdeen
February 1996

Abbreviations

AB	Anchor Bible
Bib	*Biblica*
BJRL	*Bulletin of the John Rylands University Library of Manchester*
BNTC	Black's New Testament Commentaries
CBQ	*Catholic Biblical Quarterly*
EKKNT	Evangelisch-Katholischer Kommentar zum Neuen Testament
HNT	Handbuch zum Neuen Testament
HTKNT	Herders theologischer Kommentar zum Neuen Testament
ICC	International Critical Commentary
ISBE	G.W. Bromiley (ed.), *International Standard Bible Encyclopedia*, rev. edn
JBL	*Journal of Biblical Literature*
JEH	*Journal of Ecclesiastical History*
JSNT	*Journal for the Study of the New Testament*
JTS	*Journal of Theological Studies*
MNTC	Moffatt NT Commentary
NCB	New Century Bible
NHL	Nag Hammadi Library
NICNT	New International Commentary on the New Testament
NovT	*Novum Testamentum*
NRSV	New Revised Standard Version
NTS	*New Testament Studies*
REB	Revised English Bible
WBC	Word Biblical Commentary
ZNW	*Zeitschrift für die neutestamentliche Wissenschaft*
ZTK	*Zeitschrift für Theologie und Kirche*

Commentaries and General Works on 1–3 John

Commentaries are surprisingly numerous. The following are recommended for introductory study and can be readily used by those with no knowledge of Greek:

C.H. Dodd, *The Johannine Epistles* (MNTC; London: Hodder & Stoughton, 1946). A seminal work.

K. Grayston, *The Johannine Epistles* (NCB; London: Marshall, Morgan & Scott; Grand Rapids: Eerdmans, 1984). Lively and stimulating.

J.L. Houlden, *The Johannine Epistles* (BNTC; London: A. & C. Black, 1973). Terse and scholarly.

W. Loader, *The Johannine Epistles* (Epworth Commentary; London: Epworth, 1992). Brief, simple and lively.

I.H. Marshall, *The Epistles of John* (NICNT; Grand Rapids: Eerdmans, 1978). Quite detailed and balanced.

P. Perkins, *The Johannine Epistles* (New Testament Message; Wilmington, DE: Glazier, 1979). Readable introduction.

The following contain detailed discussion of critical issues:

A.E. Brooke, *The Johannine Epistles* (ICC; Edinburgh: T. & T. Clark, 1912). Still useful.

R.E. Brown, *The Epistles of John* (AB; Garden City, NY: Doubleday, 1982). Major scholarly work, very thorough with full bibliographies.

R. Schnackenburg, *The Johannine Epistles* (HTKNT; Tunbridge Wells: Burns & Oates, ET, 1992). Full, scholarly, balanced and readable.

S.S. Smalley, *1, 2, 3 John* (WBC; Waco, TX: Word Books, 1984). Careful study; good bibliography.

Commentaries in foreign languages:

H.-J. Klauck, *Der Erste Johannesbrief* (EKKNT, 33.1; Zurich: Benziger/Neukirchener, 1991. Thorough German scholarship.

F. Vouga, *Die Johannesbriefe* (HNT 15,3; Tübingen: Mohr, 1990). Stimulating work with unusual ideas.

Basic Books and Articles:

R.E. Brown, *The Community of the Beloved Disciple* (New York: Paulist Press, 1979).

R. Bultmann, *Theology of the New Testament*, II (ET; London: SCM Press, 1955).

J.H. Charlesworth (ed.), *John and Qumran* (London: Chapman, 1972).

J.-D. Kaestli, J.-M. Poffet and J. Zumstein (eds.), *La communauté johannique et son histoire* (Geneva: Labor et Fides, 1990).

W.G. Kümmel, *The Theology of the New Testament* (ET; London: SCM Press, 1973).

—*Introduction to the New Testament* (ET; London: SCM Press, 1975).

J. Lieu, *The Theology of the Johannine Epistles* (Cambridge: Cambridge University Press, 1991).

I.H. Marshall, 'Johannine Theology' and 'John, Epistles of' in *ISBE*, II, 1982, pp. 1081-98.

These works are cited by author's name only, with date where appropriate. Further reading is given at the end of each Chapter.

1

WHY STUDY THE
JOHANNINE EPISTLES?

1. A Group of Enigmatic Writings

THE THREE EPISTLES OF JOHN occupy only five or six pages of
an English Bible, yet they are among the most intriguing
writings of the New Testament. Were they written by one
person or more? In what sort of community did they origi-
nate, and what situation are they addressing? What is the
background to their thought? How do they relate to the
Gospel of John? What is their theological message, and does
it have any relevance to the modern world? These are some
of the issues which will be considered in this Study Guide.

2. The Apostle of Love?

Saint Jerome relates an anecdote about the Apostle John:
when he grew old and infirm his disciples used to carry him
into church where he repeated again and again, 'Little children, love one another'. When asked why he always said the
same words, he replied, 'Because it is the Lord's command.
When only this is done, it is enough.' Love is certainly a
prominent theme in the Johannine writings. John's Gospel
cites Jesus' new commandment 'love one another' (Jn 13.34;
15.12, 17) three times. 1 John repeatedly stresses the need to
love: 'Little children, let us love, not in word or speech, but in
truth and action' (3.18); 'Beloved, let us love one another, for
love is from God' (4.7; cf. 4.16 etc.). The theme reappears in
2–3 John. It may indeed have been the Epistles, rather than

the Gospel, which Jerome had in mind when he recorded his famous anecdote.

Yet sensitive readers have noticed a tension between the message of love and some of the attitudes displayed. In John's Gospel the Evangelist's apparent hostility to 'the Jews' causes concern. In 1 John the problem is more with the author's attitude to those whom he calls 'antichrists' and 'deceivers' (2.18, 26). He never identifies them, but he alludes to them indirectly in polemical statements like 'Who is the liar but the one who denies that Jesus is the Christ?' (2.22). Other passages seem to refer to opponents' unsatisfactory conduct, for example, 'Whoever says, "I know him", but does not obey his commandments, is a liar' (2.4). 2 John similarly uses the terms 'deceiver' and 'Antichrist' of opponents (v. 7). Readers are warned not to receive into their house anyone who does not bring the correct teaching. Is it really showing Christian love to disparage opponents in this way, isolating them from the community? Is not dialogue more constructive than abuse?

3. Light and Darkness

The reason for the apparent gap between the splendid Johannine teaching on love and the stern condemnation of those who do not share the same understanding of the faith lies in belief in an absolute distinction between truth and falsehood. For the Johannine author(s) these are exact opposites, totally incompatible with one another. They are as different as light and darkness—a frequent metaphor in these writings. At the start of 1 John the author proclaims: 'This is the message which we have heard from him and announce to you, that God is light and in him there is no darkness at all' (1.5). He also speaks of 'walking in the light' and 'walking in the darkness'. These polarized opposites—light/darkness, truth/falsehood, good/evil, 'of the world'/'not of the world', Christ/Antichrist, God/Devil, life/death—reveal a dualistic world-view in which everything is seen as black or white. There are no half-truths, no shades of grey. As Bultmann (1955) among others has stressed, this 'dualism' is characteristic of the whole Johannine corpus. There are parallels to this mode of thought in the Qumran texts (Dead Sea Scrolls), in other Jewish and New Testament writings, and in Gnosticism, which we shall be exploring later. A dualistic framework also undergirds Revelation, though the light/darkness imagery is not so strong there.

Pedagogically these opposites are important. In an urgent situation, if you want to persuade someone to do what is right or to believe what you hold to be true, it is no use hedging your views round with numerous qualifications. You need to be clear-cut and decisive. This is exactly what the author of 1 John is. He knows what he believes to be right and true, and he states it clearly and decisively. But such confident attitudes can also cause problems.

4. Them and Us

One problem is that such attitudes tend to polarise people as well as ideas. Groups and individuals are categorized as 'true believers' or 'heretics'. You are either 'in' or 'out'. In recent years scholars such as R.E. Brown and W.A. Meeks have criticized the Johannine writings as 'sectarian'. A key verse is 1 Jn 2.19, 'They went out from us, but they were not of us; for if they had been of us, they would have remained with us'. These dissidents are condemned as belonging to 'the world' and contrasted with those of orthodox faith: 'What they say is of the world, and the world listens to them. We are of God; whoever knows God listens to us' (4.6). In other words, 'We are right, and they are wrong'.

This raises a further question about the Johannine concept of love. Is it a *universal* love, or only for those within the accepted circle? Judaism taught the need to love one's 'neighbour' (usually understood as 'fellow-Jew'). It was considered acceptable to hate one's enemies (e.g. Ps. 139.21-22). By contrast Jesus, according to the Synoptics, taught love of enemies and redefined the meaning of 'neighbour' to include even Samaritans. When in John's Gospel Jesus commands his followers to love 'one another', many scholars see this as narrowing the love command to believers. In 1 John Jesus' teaching on love also seems to be restricted. It is expressed in terms of loving *tous adelphous* (literally, 'the brothers'),

which the NRSV renders inclusively as 'brothers and sisters'
and the REB as 'fellow-Christians'. But who are these 'brothers'? Are they all humanity, or just Christians? Or only one
group within those who would claim to be Christian? And
does the author really intend 'brothers' to include 'women'?

For many readers the seemingly negative attitude to the
world also raises difficulties. 1 John warns, 'Do not love the
world or the things in the world' (2.16). Are we not meant to
love God's good creation? The problem is that the Johannine
writings use the term *ho kosmos* ('the world') with more than
one meaning. In John's Gospel it is sometimes used quite
positively in the sense of the created order, which is loved by
God (Jn 3.16); but it is also used of people in opposition to
God, who are seen as belonging to 'this world', and not having 'eternal life'. Sometimes these two different meanings are
used in the same sentence: 'He was in the world, and the
world was made through him; yet the world did not know
him' (Jn 1.10). The danger with this ambivalent usage is that
all too easily the phrase 'the world' can be taken as implying
that God's creation is evil, or that material things in general
are bad (as happened in Gnosticism). In 1–3 John the problem is even more acute than in John's Gospel, as positive
uses of 'the world' are almost lacking, and teaching is given
which might readily foster negative attitudes to God's material gifts: 'The love of the Father is not in those who love the
world; for all that is in the world—the desire of the flesh, the
desire of the eyes, the boastfulness of life—comes not from
the Father but from the world' (1 Jn 2.16-17). This world is
said to be passing away, whereas those who do God's will live
for ever. Here we are close to the concepts of those Jewish
thinkers who sharply contrasted this 'world' or 'age' (Hebrew
haʿolam hazzeh has both meanings) with the 'world' or 'age' to
come. Taken to an extreme these ways of thought lead to
intolerance, an 'otherworldly' withdrawal from society, and
rigorous asceticism. But can they also have more positive
effects?

5. Right Behaviour and Right Belief

How does one decide who are 'inside' the community and who are not? Two criteria appear to be used, one ethical, the other doctrinal. (a) The ethical criterion concerns love and right behaviour. 'Whoever says "I am in the light", while hating a "brother", is still in darkness' (1 Jn 2.9); 'Everyone who hates their "brother" is a murderer' (3.15). In contrast, those who refuse to love 'the world' are acceptable. Similarly, 'everyone who does what is right is righteous', while 'everyone who commits sin is a child of the devil' (3.7-8). Sometimes these twin ethical criteria of love and right conduct are combined in a single affirmation: 'The children of God and the children of the devil are revealed in this way: all who do not do what is right are not from God, nor are those who do not love their "brothers"' (3.10). 3 John sets out similar tests: 'Whoever does good is from God: whoever does evil has not seen God' (3 Jn 11). But who defines 'what is right'? And what about those who sometimes do right, and sometimes wrong? Or those who love most of the time, but sometimes fall short?

(b) The second test is right belief: 'Every spirit that confesses Jesus Christ come in the flesh is from God, and every spirit that does not confess Jesus is not from God' (4.2; cf. 2.22; 4.15; 5.1). Similarly 2 Jn 7 states that those who do not confess Jesus Christ coming in the flesh are 'the deceiver and the Antichrist'. Precisely what is meant by these phrases about 'confessing' Jesus Christ? Several of the statements are ambiguous in the Greek and many different solutions have been put forward as to the identity of the 'deceivers'. But even if we knew exactly who they were, it would still be difficult to apply such teaching today. With our imperfect knowledge of God, who can define what is truth and what is falsehood? Testing by confession of 'the truth' leads all too easily into the perils of heresy-hunting. At the same time, in a world which has experienced Nazism, apartheid, and many other kinds of religious and ethnic oppression, one is acutely aware of the wickedness perpetrated by those who substitute good for evil in their sense of values. Surely we can look to the Bible for guidance concerning truth and falsehood?

6. Do Believers Sin?

In defining any dogmatic belief it is difficult to ensure that one's statements are both logical and unambiguous—a point to which compilers of ecumenical 'Agreed Statements' would readily assent. All too often what we say is misunderstood by someone who reads or hears it without sharing our presuppositions or immediate concerns. Such problems become even more acute with a hortatory text designed to inculcate certain attitudes or effect a particular form of conduct. What may seem perfectly clear and logical to the author(s), may not seem so to the readers. This is especially true if the reader is distanced from the original author(s) by time, space, or culture, as we are from the Johannine Epistles.

These contain theological tensions and ambiguities which pose difficulties for the modern reader eager to discover their true meaning. A particular problem concerns 1 John's teaching on sin. In the first two chapters the author clearly envisages the possibility that those to whom he is writing are capable of sinning: 'If anyone sins, we have an advocate with the Father, Jesus Christ the righteous' (2.1). Yet he goes on to say, 'Nobody who abides in him sins; nobody who sins has seen or known him' (3.6). The first part of this sentence might possibly be taken to mean that when Christians sin, they break their fellowship with Christ. But the second part clearly states that those who sin have *never* known Christ. The logical conundrum in reconciling this with the statement 'If we say we have no sin, we deceive ourselves' (1.8) is made even more difficult by the following verses: 'Everyone who commits sin is from the devil...*nobody born from God commits sin*' (3.8-9). Quite apart from the tension with earlier statements, this stands against the evidence of Christian experience. Is the author confused? Is he uncritically combining different sources? Can the words bear another meaning? Or is the apparent contradiction to be explained by the writer's rhetorical purpose? These and other theological questions will be discussed later, but meanwhile we need to consider a method for pursuing this enquiry.

7. Methodology

Since Bultmann—if not before—scholars have been aware that there is no such thing as 'presuppositionless exegesis'. We are all children of our time, products of particular social and educational systems, and are influenced, whether we recognise it or not, by our upbringing, our intellectual and religious convictions (or non-convictions), and possibly adherence to, or rebellion against, a particular denominational background. While we can never divorce ourselves from these factors—indeed many would hold it is wrong to try to do so—we need to be aware of them and to have a conscious methodology in studying a text.

Through the centuries there have been many different approaches to the interpretation of the Johannine Epistles. In the Church Fathers one finds them used for controversial, doctrinal and devotional purposes. For example, Irenaeus uses 1–2 John's denunciations of 'antichrists' to encourage true belief and the forsaking of 'false' teaching. Clement of Alexandria and Tertullian use 1 Jn 5.16-17 to discuss different kinds of sin. Augustine draws freely on 1 John to promote the ideal of Christian love; Cyprian to urge ethical conduct. From the earliest citations we find the Johannines (especially 1 John) treated as Scripture. It is assumed that the writings are inspired and their teachings to be adopted. Some Fathers show an awareness of what we would call critical issues. Dionysius of Alexandria is famous for separating the authorship of John's Gospel and the Apocalypse; Jerome reports the view that 2-3 John are by an 'Elder' rather than John the Evangelist. But the Fathers were mostly concerned with dogmatic issues, and with encouraging Church members to live holy lives.

In patristic writing 1–3 John tend to be overshadowed by the Gospel of John, envisaged as the work of a preacher of sublime truth who soared up to heaven like an eagle (so Augustine). But there was a source of concern: John's Gospel was very early adopted by Gnostics like Ptolemaeus and Valentinus, who built up elaborate systems drawing on the syncretistic thought of Greece and the East, couching their ideas in language quite close to that of the Gospel. This led to suspicions about its orthodoxy, and sometimes 1 John was used by orthodox Fathers to defend it.

In the Medieval and Reformation periods the Johannines seem again to have been mostly used for devotional, dogmatic, and controversial purposes. It is not until post-enlightenment times that one finds the first serious critical scholarship, especially in Germany. It is beyond our scope to discuss the development of modern scholarship, but it is probably fair to say that until around the 1970s the main concerns were with historical, theological and literary-critical issues. What is the genre of 1–3 John? Can one identify written sources? Did the same author write John's Gospel and the Epistles? Are there differences in language, style and theology between these writings? Who are the 'opponents' of 1 and 2 John? What ecclesiastical situation do the Johannines presuppose? There has, for example, been considerable interest in Germany over the question of 'Frühkatholizismus' (early Catholicism), and whether the presbyter of 2–3 John is a Bishop. In the 1950–70s there was also a strong interest in 'Biblical Theology'—an attempt to bring the Bible's doctrinal and ethical teaching into a coherent pattern. Scholars focused on the 'theology' of individual authors or groups of writings, e.g. the Pauline letters; the Johannine writings. Sometimes Revelation was considered alongside John's Gospel and 1–3 John; more often it was treated separately. Most scholars treated the theology of the Johannine Gospel and Epistles as a unity, including Kümmel, Guthrie, Bultmann and Marshall—to name a few notable figures. An outstanding exception was Dodd, who as early as the 1930s had argued for separate authorship of these writings on theological as well as linguistic grounds.

Those who practised such historical-critical scholarship might be 'liberals' or 'conservatives', and they differed widely in their conclusions. But their methods were basically the same. More recently, scholarship has begun to separate even further the various Johannine writings. Judith Lieu in *The Theology of the Johannine Epistles* (1991) argues that they must be allowed in speak in their own right rather than under the shadow of the Gospel; both she and Kenneth Grayston have suggested that more than one author may be involved in the composition of 1–3 John.

New methods and issues have also emerged. Following the work of scholars like Malherbe, Theissen and Meeks, there has been a surge of interest in the social background of the Epistles. In *The Community of the Beloved Disciple* (1979), followed by his massive Anchor Bible Commentary (1982), Raymond Brown has put forward an elaborate conjectural history of the community which he believes to lie behind both Gospel and Epistles, and the loves and hates of its members. Particularly in North America, but also in Britain, there has been a lively interest in the question of whether this community was a 'sect'. The Johannines' teaching on Christology and love, once piously accepted at its face-value, has come in for much criticism.

Partly as a reaction against the negative and 'atomizing' character of some historical-critical scholarship, recent decades have seen the rise of new types of criticism in which practitioners have sought to look at the biblical writings holistically, and to be more aware of their functions as 'text'. Scholars such as H.-J. Klauck, F. Vouga, and D.F. Watson are now applying 'rhetorical criticism' to the Johannines, and D. Neufeld has recently published an analysis of 1 John based on speech-act theory (1994). Structuralist, post-structuralist, and semiotic interpretative methods have not yet hit our texts, though these and other modern 'criticisms' are being applied to John's Gospel. Side by side with these new approaches, study by traditional methods is continued by both conservative and radical scholars. Thus Johannine studies are in a creative state of flux.

8. Approach of this Book

The basic approach of this book is historical-critical. It considers such issues as sources, authorship, literary unity, style, genre and milieu as objectively as possible. At the same time, starting with the shorter Epistles, it seeks to understand the Johannines as literary wholes, with an awareness of their rhetorical purpose and effects on readers/hearers. Rather than treating the Epistles in their canonical order, the study will begin with 3 and 2 John. I do this because their form and contents are relatively straight-forward and easy to grasp, and I treat 3 John first, since I believe that it was written before 2 John. After this we turn to the most challenging Epistle, namely 1 John, which raises a bigger range of interesting ideas.

A special focus of this study will be the Johannines' theological content—for it is as *theological* writings, rather than as 'great literature', that most modern readers study these texts. We shall therefore need to evaluate their teachings and presuppositions in such key areas as Christology and ethics. Our aim is to let the Epistles speak in their own right, without positing any particular relation to John's Gospel. But inevitably comparisons must be drawn with other books of the New Testament, not only because parts of 1 John, in particular, cannot be understood without some reference to them, but also because such comparisons are valuable in their own right. It will also be helpful to refer to the Johannines' wider background in the Hebrew Bible and contemporary Jewish and Graeco-Roman writings.

In all this readers should bear in mind that 1–3 John, like the rest of the New Testament, are written in Greek. Many students suppose their language is easy, since their range of vocabulary and grammatical constructions is small; in fact, the Greek of 1 John is in many places ambiguous and obscure. Most translations—and even some commentaries—gloss over the difficulties. In the present study it is possible to discuss only a few of the controversial passages, but it is hoped that readers will be stimulated to explore further their detailed exegesis for themselves.

Finally, I hope to share with readers my own commitment to the Christian faith, and the belief that we can learn something of value from these writings, though one should not accept their message uncritically. In the final chapter I shall attempt to assess something of their strengths and weaknesses, and discover some message for the world today.

Further Reading

Composition and Authorship:
Introductions to commentaries by Brown, Dodd, Houlden, Marshall.
D. Guthrie, *New Testament Introduction* (London: Inter-Varsity Press, rev. edn, 1970), ch. 26.
Kümmel 1975: §31.

Theology:
Bultmann 1955.
Kümmel 1973.
Marshall 1982b.
Lieu 1991.

Community and Sectarianism:
Brown 1979.
B.S. Childs, *The New Testament as Canon* (London: SCM Press, 1984), pp. 482-85.

Rhetorical Criticism:
H.-J. Klauck, 'Zur rhetorischen Analyse der Johannesbriefe', *ZNW* 81 (1990), pp. 205-24.
D. Neufeld, *Reconceiving Texts as Speech Acts: An Analysis of 1 John* (Leiden: Brill, 1994).
F. Vouga, 'La réception de la théologie johannique dans les épîtres', in Kaestli 1990: 283-302.
D.F. Watson and A.J. Hauser, *Rhetorical Criticism of the Bible* (Leiden: Brill, 1994).

2

2 AND 3 JOHN:
FORM, STYLE AND CONTENT

1. Types of Letter in the Ancient World

THE GRAECO-ROMAN WORLD knew many different kinds of epistolary writing. There were short philosophical treatises in the form of letters, like the Epistles of Epicurus; fictional letters written as creative literary exercises; official letters reporting on events or asking for advice; pastoral and ecclesiastical letters, like those of Paul in the New Testament and Ignatius and Polycarp in the Apostolic Fathers. And there were private letters, sometimes quite literary, like Cicero's letters to his friends, sometimes informal and almost illiterate, like the thousands of letters on papyri dealing with business matters and domestic affairs. It is helpful to have these different categories in mind in considering the literary form of 1–3 John.

The private letters are most relevant to 2 and 3 John. Many of these take a regular form: (a) greeting in the third person singular; (b) a wish for good health for the recipient; (c) main body, often containing a request; (d) sometimes a reference to a possible meeting; (e) final greetings and wishes for good health. The following is a typical example:

> Dromon to Zenon greetings. We give thanks to all the gods if you are in good health yourself and everything else is in good order. We too are well, and in accordance with your instructions I am taking every care that no one troubles your people. When you are well enough to sail up (the Nile), order one of your people to buy a measure of Attic honey; for I need it for my eyes by order of the god. Keep well (PCairo Zen. 59426, 3rd century BCE).

2. The Form, Style and Content of 3 John

3 John begins with a greeting in the third person, 'The Elder to the beloved Gaius' (v. 1) followed by a wish for good health and expression of pleasure (vv. 2-4). Next the author praises Gaius and requests him to send some 'brothers' on their way worthily of God. The author refers to a previous letter (as commonly in such correspondence); mentions a man called Diotrephes who is causing problems, and promises a visit to sort things out. He commends a certain Demetrius, expresses his hope of seeing Gaius in person, wishes him peace, and sends greetings from friends.

Of all the writings in the New Testament, 3 John conforms most closely to the pattern of a private letter such as the papyrus example just cited. It is short—only 185 words— shorter than any of Paul's letters, but about the same length as some of Cicero's shorter letters. It would fit comfortably on to a single sheet of papyrus. It is concerned with a specific problem. It may well have been conveyed to Gaius by the Demetrius who is so warmly commended (cf. 1 Pet. 5.12, commending its bearer Silvanus; also Cicero, *Ad Fam.* 1.3).

At the same time there are some peculiarities: (a) the author's name is not given, but only his title, 'the Elder'. This may indicate that he is writing in his capacity of a church leader, rather than purely personally. (b) The regular word for 'greetings' (*chairein*) is missing from the opening saluta- tion. The omission of a word for greeting is not uncommon in Aramaic letters, but very rare in Greek ones. (c) The health wish takes an unusual form: the author prays that Gaius is keeping in good physical health, as he is well in his *psychē* (life, spirit or soul). This makes a distinction between Gaius's bodily and spiritual health. (d) There are a few peculiar turns of expression in the Greek. (e) Instead of the usual 'keep well' at the end of the letter, it has 'peace'. This corre- sponds to the Jewish greeting *shalom*, extremely common in Aramaic letters. Other semitic turns of expression include 'walk' in the sense of 'behave' (v. 3) and 'mouth to mouth' for 'face to face' (v. 14).

The letter uses many phrases familiar from secular letters, for example, 'I was very pleased', 'you will do well' (often associated with a request). It also contains some specifically Jewish-Christian vocabulary: 'the congregation' (*ecclēsia*), 'gentiles', 'fellow-workers', 'children' (for the addressees), 'the Name', and 'brothers' in the sense of a religious community. In places the phraseology is reminiscent of John's Gospel and 1 John, for example, the references to 'seeing God' and being 'of God' (v. 11; cf. Jn 1.18; 1 Jn 4.4, etc.) and the themes of 'witness' (5×), 'truth' (6×) and 'love' (6×)—a remarkable number of occurrences for such a short letter. Note especially v. 12b, 'and you know that our witness is true' (cf. Jn 21.24); 'the friends' (v. 15; cf. Jn 15.14-15). It is possible that the Elder, as pastor, is deliberately echoing Jesus' words from the Johannine tradition. The striking personification of truth in v. 12 may recall Jn 15.26-27 (the spirit of truth as witness). 'Peace' as a greeting reminds us of Jesus' greeting in Jn 20.19, 26, though it could be just a Christian form of the regular Jewish greeting (cf. Paul's usage).

The main business of the letter, as Malherbe (1977) has argued, is *hospitality*. In the ancient world where inns were few and unreliable most travellers used private hospitality. Sometimes people entertained complete strangers (cf. Abraham's proverbial welcoming of angels). Those who shared religious beliefs often gave hospitality to one another, but there was always a risk of being imposed on. It is evident from 3 John that travelling brothers whom Gaius (a common Latin name) had not known personally had visited him, and taken back good reports to the Elder. The Elder warmly commends Gaius for his generosity to strangers who came 'in the Name', since they had been able to rely entirely on Christian hospitality without taking anything from pagans. He urges him to continue such action, so that they may become 'fellow-workers with the truth'. The motivation is theological rather than personal.

Next the Elder deals with the inhospitable Diotrephes. He complains that Diotrephes 'is hungry for power' (lit. 'likes the pre-eminence'); he does not receive the Elder, and he talks nonsense about him. Not content with that, Diotrephes has declined to receive the 'brothers' and has expelled them. There has been much debate about Diotrephes' ecclesial role. Some have thought that he was an early monarchic bishop, either 'orthodox' or 'heretical'. But if Diotrephes is a bishop, why is the Elder interfering in his area of jurisdiction? Is there not a danger of reading into this text later forms of Church government?

The nature of the Elder's dispute with Diotrephes has also been much debated. There seems no reason to view it as doctrinal: no doctrinal issues are mentioned. Some believe that the issue is *authority*, understanding *ouk epidechetai* in v. 9 as 'does not accept our authority' and *ekballō* ('expel') and *kōlyō* ('hinder') in v. 10 in the technical ecclesiastical sense of 'excommunicate' and 'forbid'. But *epidechetai* can mean just 'receive hospitably' (cf. v. 10), and the other words are more plausibly understood as 'decline' to receive someone in one's house and 'not permit' other members of a house-church to do so. Nor does the verb *phlyareō* ('talk nonsense') mean 'bring charges against', but rather 'gossip maliciously' (cf. 1 Tim. 5.13). The dispute, then, seems to be about church hospitality rather than doctrine or authority. We are dealing with a pastoral and moral, rather than ecclesiastical, issue (so Stott).

What of the Elder's own status? There is no hint that he is an apostle; but if he is only a local church leader, why does he write so authoritatively to a member of another congregation? Perhaps he is relying on greater seniority in the faith, or presuming on his personal relationship to Diotrephes and Gaius. We note the references to mutual friends, the promise of a visit, and the implication that Gaius is one of his 'children' or protégés. Whatever the circumstances, the Elder is in a position to commend, censure and exhort: Gaius is praised for his Christian behaviour and his hospitality; Diotrephes is held up as a model of how *not* to behave. In all this 3 John follows a common pattern of rhetoric designed to earn goodwill, assign praise and blame, and affect the behaviour of others (cf. Watson 1989b). The author's generous attitude over hospitality to fellow-Christians is remarkable. No conditions are laid down; no limits on length of stay (contrast the *Didache*); no doctrinal safeguards. Even strangers should be received who come 'for the sake of the Name'. One is reminded of Jesus' teaching: 'Freely you have received; freely give' (Mt. 10.8).

3. 2 John: Opening Address and the 'Elect Lady'

2 John follows the same structure as 3 John. There is a greeting from the Elder to the recipients (vv. 1-3), a reference to his joy (v. 4), and a request (v. 5), leading to the main business—a warning against 'deceivers' (vv. 6-11). The author expresses a wish to visit the recipients, and sends greetings (vv. 12-13). There are, however, differences. The letter is not addressed to a named man, but to 'an elect lady and her children' (we shall return to this enigmatic greeting later).

The prescript contains other unusual features. Instead of the simple health wish, we have an elaborate 'ecclesiastical' greeting, 'There will be with us grace, mercy, peace, from Father God and from Jesus Christ, the Son of the Father, in truth and love'. The form is similar to the specifically Christian greetings in other New Testament letters where *charis* ('grace') is substituted for secular *chairein* ('rejoice'). 'Peace' also occurs in other New Testament letters, taken over from Jewish greetings; 'mercy' is less common (but note 1 Tim. 1.1; 2 Tim. 1.1; Jude 1). There are, however, peculiarities in the Elder's formulation. (a) He does not identify himself by name (cf. 3 John); (b) the formal greeting comes in a separate sentence from the opening address; (c) it is a statement rather than a wish (contrast 1–2 Peter, Paul and the Apostolic Fathers). It looks as if v. 3 has been awkwardly added to a simpler greeting. Observe also the curious juxtaposition of favourite Johannine vocabulary—'love', 'truth', 'abide' (vv. 1-2)—with untypical vocabulary (v. 3), notably *charis* (only once in John's Gospel, never in 1 John), 'mercy' (not elsewhere in Johannine literature), the un-Johannine 'Father God' (lacking the article with 'God' and the modifier 'our'), and the peculiar, quasi-liturgical, description of Jesus as 'the Son of the Father'. Yet v. 3 also uses typical Johannine vocabulary in the phrase 'in truth and love', tacked on to the Pauline-style greeting. The most probable explanation is that the author himself added this rather grand 'apostolic' greeting to give his letter more theological weight and to emphasise the concepts of truth and love so dear to him.

We turn now to the problem of the 'Elect Lady' (*eklektē*

kyria, with no word for 'the'). There is no exact parallel to this designation in biblical or secular Greek. Most modern commentators suppose the phrase is used metaphorically for a church. In the Hebrew Bible, Jerusalem or Zion is often personified as a woman; sometimes Israel is pictured as God's bride—imagery occasionally picked up in the New Testament (cf. Rev. 21.2; Eph. 5.25-28). In the *Shepherd of Hermas*, a second-century CE allegorical writing, the Church appears as a woman in a vision and is addressed by the author as *kyria*. But there are major differences between these images and 2 John's. In Revelation, Ephesians and *Hermas* it is the new Jerusalem or the Church *as a whole* which is personified, not one congregation. Yet if the 'elect lady' of v. 1 is the whole Church, who is her 'elect sister' in v. 13?

Examples of a local church personified as a woman are not frequent: several commentators cite 2 Cor. 11.2, Tertullian, *Ad Martyras* 1.1 and 1 Pet. 5.13 in this connection. But the first two authors make it abundantly clear that they are writing figuratively: Paul wishes to present the Corinthian Christians to Christ '*like* a pure virgin'; Tertullian (writing in North Africa c. 200 CE) speaks of 'lady mother *church*' *(domina mater ecclesia)* providing from her bountiful breasts for prisoners. In neither case is the word *eklektē* used. 1 Pet. 5.13 provides the closest parallel in *hē en Babylōni syneklektē* 'the co-elect (woman) in Babylon'. It is usually assumed that *syneklektē* here means the church at Rome; but it is possible that it refers to an individual woman (so Bigg, ICC, 1910).

Could *eklektē kyria* in 2 Jn 1 also be taken in its more natural sense of a real woman? Four possible interpretations have been put forward: (a) (*Kyria* might be a proper name, and *eklektē* an adjective (ancient Greek did not use capitals to indicate proper nouns); (b) *Kyria* might be an adjective and *Eklektē* a proper name; (c) both *Kyria* and *Eklektē* might be proper names; (d) perhaps neither is a proper name. We consider each hypothesis briefly in turn.

(a) *Kyria*, meaning 'mistress', 'lady' (cf. Aramaic 'Martha') is found as a personal name in both inscriptions and papyri; *eklektē*, meaning 'chosen', or 'elect' (of God) is an appropriate epithet for a Christian leader (cf. Rom. 16.13. Rufus, the elect in the Lord; Ignatius, *Phil.* 11.1. Rheus Agathopous, an elect man). It has been objected that one might expect the definite article with *eklektē*. We can reply that this letter is not written in fully idiomatic Greek, having other linguistic peculiarities (cf. the occurrence of 'Father' both with and without the article in v. 3); if *eklektē kyria* means 'the Church' the absence of the article is also odd.

(b) In favour of *kyria* as a common noun is its frequent appearance in the papyri as a polite and affectionate form of address to an older woman (cf. P. Oxy 744, 'to Berous my lady', etc). Against this has been argued the absence of 'my' with *Kyria* and lack of evidence for *Eklektē* as a personal name in contemporary papyri (so Brown 1982: 653). Indeed Findlay alleged that '*Eklektē* occurs nowhere else in Greek...as a proper name' (1909: 23). One may reply that 'my' is not always found with *kyria* in the papyri, and although the name *Eklektē* has not so far been found in the papyri, it is attested in Greek inscriptions, along with a parallel male name *Eklektos* (known also in literary sources). We may mention also a series of inscriptions of imperial date from Rome with the woman's name *Eclecte* or *Eglecte* (c. 7×). Although the inscriptions are in Latin, the form of this name is Greek. The idea that *Eklektē* might be a personal name also receives some support from Clement of Alexandria, who thought that 2 John was written to 'a certain Babylonian woman called Electa' (according to the *Adumbrationes*, a Latin translation of his *Hypotyposes*).

A problem often raised with understanding *Eklektē* as a proper name is its reappearance at v. 13. Mention of two women with the same name in such a short letter might seem improbable, but the ancient world had a smaller range of women's names than we do (cf. all the New Testament Marys). The woman in v. 13 need not be a blood sister; she may equally well be a Christian sister, herself a church leader. Alternatively *eklektē* in v. 13 could be the adjective 'elect'. It might seem awkward to use the same Greek word both as a proper name and as an adjective within 13 verses, but ancient writers were not so sensitive to such grammatical distinctions as modern ones; the repetition of *eklektē* in v. 13 must deliberately echo v. 1, and it is likely the two women shared a common role. Incidentally, the final greetings are not from the 'elect sister' herself, but from her children. If this is a real woman, she must be either deceased or at least not present with the writer. In either case it is hard to believe she is a church.

(c) The idea that both *Kyria* and *Eklektē* might be proper names is described by Westcott as 'very strange', but such double names are common in the ancient world, and *Eclecte* occurs combined with other personal names in the Roman inscriptions mentioned.

(d) The case for the 'elect lady' as a real woman does not stand or fall on taking *Kyria* or *Eklektē* (or both) as a proper name. 'Chosen lady' could equally well be a sobriquet (or nickname), like the Gospel of John's 'disciple whom Jesus loved', for someone whom the author, for whatever reason, did not wish to name directly. One sometimes suspects that a reason why the 'elect lady' has been so rarely taken as an individual is reluctance to assume that a woman could have led a church. But female church leaders are attested elsewhere in the New Testament: we note particularly 'Nympha and the Church at her house' (Col. 4.15) and Phoebe, minister or deacon of the Church at Cenchreae (Rom. 16.1). Thus our *eklektē kyria* may well have hosted or led a local congregation; 'her children', to whom the letter is also addressed, were probably not her physical children, but rather members of her house-church. Thus the letter is still written to a church even if the 'elect lady' is taken to be an individual.

4. 2 John: Main Body

What is the basic purport of 2 John? The Elder says that he loves the 'elect lady and her children' in truth (using the same phraseology as 3 Jn 1). He says that not only he loves them, but so do 'all who know the truth', because of 'the truth that abides in us'. The linking of love and truth is striking. The phrase '*all* who know the truth' is either hyperbole (cf. Rom. 1.8, when Paul says that the faith of the Roman Christians is talked of over the *whole* world), or, more probably, an exclusive claim to know the truth on behalf of the author and his community. Next the Elder rejoices that he has found some of the lady's children walking in the truth. Functionally this sentence, like the opening one, is a *captatio benevolentiae*, to win the goodwill of the recipients (cf. 3 Jn 3). But the tone may be less warm than in 3 John if only *some* of the lady's children walk in the truth.

The Elder then moves on to his main agenda, marked by a repeated address to the 'lady' (*kyria*)—vocatives are common in the papyri at this point—and the typical verb *erōtaō*, 'ask'. But instead of the usual request for a favour, we have an exhortation to mutual love. The author assures the lady that he is not writing 'a new commandment, but one which we had from the beginning' (the vocabulary is Johannine: cf. *entolē*, 'commandment', 14× in 1 Jn; 11× John's Gospel). But the sentence is phrased awkwardly: one would expect a second person verb, 'I request you, lady, that you...', not a first person plural ('we'). One would also expect a specific request rather than theological exhortation. The phraseology seems to be modelled on 1 John, where the author writes, 'This is the commandment which we had from the beginning that we love one another' (3.11) and 'Beloved, I do not write a new commandment to you, but an old commandment which you had from the beginning' (2.7). 'From the beginning' is a favourite phrase of 1 John (8×) and is indicative of the author's harking back to the foundations of Christianity.

Next, the Elder defines love: 'This is love, that we walk according to his commandments' (v. 6a). The structure, 'This is *x*', followed by a 'that' clause, or another noun, is a favourite in 1 John (e.g. 1.5; 3.11; cf. Jn 15.12; 17.3). The remarkable point is that love is defined entirely in terms of keeping God's (or Christ's) command—a thought found also in 1 John. Another definition follows, exactly parallel in syntax: 'This is the command, as you heard from the beginning, that you walk in it' (v. 6b). Note again the characteristic phrase 'from the beginning', harking back to origins. It is ambiguous whether 'in it' (a feminine pronoun in the Greek) refers to the 'commandment' or 'love', or even to 'truth'. But it makes little difference to the sense. The phrase seems rather repetitive, but it serves to stress the significance the author attaches to love, truth and obedience.

He now speaks of some who have presumably failed in

these areas—deceivers who 'have gone out into the world' (another Johannine phrase: cf. 1 Jn 4.1)—who does not confess Jesus Christ 'coming in the flesh'. These deceivers are defined (vv. 7-8) as 'the deceiver and the Antichrist' (using the same formula, 'this is...', in spite of the plural antecedent). The vocabulary is Johannine, including the use of 'confess' with a personal object (cf. Jn 9.22; 1 Jn 2.23, etc.), 'antichrist' (unique to the Johannine writings in the New Testament: cf. 1 Jn 2.18, 22; 4.3), and reference to Jesus 'coming in the flesh' (cf. 1 Jn 4.2). The 'deceiver' reminds us of 'those who deceive you' in 1 Jn 2.26 (cf. Rev. 12.9; also 1 Tim. 4.1). The content also is very close to the thought of 1 John, where we have the same idea that those who do not make the right christological confession are God's archetypal spiritual enemy. The seriousness of such an allegation should not be underestimated. But who are guilty of this terrible act? They may be the same group as are denounced in 1 John for denying Jesus' incarnation (assuming that is the meaning of 2 John's ambiguous phrase here: see Chapter 8 §3).

The author also warns his addressees to be on their guard that they do not lose what has been achieved. For everyone who 'goes ahead' (*proagō*) and does not abide in Christ's teaching does not 'have' the Father or the Son. This is the only place in the New Testament where *proagō* (an un-Johannine word) is used in a metaphorical sense. It is evident that the author is a conservative Christian, nervous of 'progressives' who (in his view) go beyond the basic teaching of (or about) Jesus. His is not the spirit of intellectual enquiry or innovative theology, but rather of faithfulness to what he has received. So serious does he deem departing from this tradition that he forbids the Elect Lady and her children greet them or give them hospitality, because to do so would be to share in their evil deeds. This is a far cry from the generous, condition-free hospitality of 3 John. Either the situation has drastically changed, or we are dealing with a different author. ?

So we reach the end of the letter. The author says that having many other things to write, he does not wish to use paper and ink; he would rather speak personally to his addressees, 'so that our joy may be full'. The sentence parallels the end of 3 John, though there the author says 'pen and ink'. References to writing materials are exceedingly rare at the end of papyrus letters. This raises the possibility of a direct imitation of 3 John by 2 John, as is also suggested by the complicated syntax in v. 12. The 'extreme joy' at the prospect of a meeting seems out of place in a letter sparked by a doctrinal crisis. The phrase is virtually identical to the one used more appropriately in the opening of 1 John. Is this another sign that 2 John is imitative?

5. Conclusion

We conclude that, while there is no reason doubt that 3 John is a genuine private letter, 2 John is more problematic. Though clearly in letter form, it has more specifically 'Christian' features, including the lengthy prescript. It has a less engaging and less direct style than 3 John, and is obscure in places. Bultmann and others have suggested that it might be an artificial compilation in imitation of 3 John. If so, its purpose would be to claim the authority of the 'Elder' (presumably a well-known figure) to refute 'heresy'. We know that 1 and 2 John were used for this purpose in the patristic Church, just as 3 John was used to urge bishops to be hospitable. But the conjecture lacks proof. An alternative might be to see it still as secondary to 3 John, but a genuine letter by a church leader who was also a presbyter/elder. A third alternative is to regard the letters as the work of one man, but to explain the differences in style as due to their having different purposes. The lack of clarity might arise from old age, or from the fact that the author was not a native Greek speaker. Both letters contain semitizing vocabulary, and 2 John also shows features of semitic syntax (esp. v. 2, where a participial clause with the verb 'abiding' is resolved into a main clause with an indicative verb). All this may have some bearing on authorship, which will be the theme of Chapter 4.

Further Reading

J.R.W. Stott, *The Epistles of John* (Leicester: Inter-Varsity Press, 1964).

R. Bultmann, *The Johannine Epistles* (ET; Hermeneia; Philadelphia: Fortress Press, 1973).

J. Lieu, *The Second and Third Epistles of John* (Edinburgh: T. & T. Clark, 1986) (detailed study).

On Form and Style:

R.W. Funk, 'The Form and Structure of II and III John', *JBL* 86 (1967), pp. 424-30.

J.L. White, 'The Greek Documentary Letter Tradition Third Century BCE to Third Century CE', in *Studies in Ancient Letter Writing* = *Semeia* 22 (1981), pp. 89-106.

D.F. Watson, 'A Rhetorical Analysis of 2 John according to Greco-Roman Convention', *NTS* 35 (1989), pp. 104-30.

—'A Rhetorical Analysis of 3 John: A Study in Epistolary Rhetoric', *CBQ* 51 (1989), pp. 479-501.

On the Church Situation:

A.J. Malherbe, 'The Inhospitality of Diotrephes', in J. Jervell and W.A. Meeks (eds.), *God's Christ and his People* (FS Dahl; Oslo: Universitetsforlaget, 1977), pp. 222-32.

E. Schweizer, *Church Order in the New Testament* (ET; London: SCM Press, 1961), ch. 12.

On the 'Elect Lady':

Brown 1982.

Grayston.

Marshall.

Schnackenburg.

G.G. Findlay, *Fellowship in the Life Eternal* (London: Hodder & Stoughton, 1909).

B.F. Westcott, *The Epistles of St John* (London: Macmillan, 4th edn, 1902 (taking as a personification).

Ramsay and Deissmann in Brown 1982: 652-54.

L. Morris in *New Bible Commentary: Revised* (London: Inter-Varsity Press, 1970), p. 1271.

D.R. Pape, *God and Woman* (Oxford: Mowbray, 1977), p. 206 (taking as individual woman).

3

1 JOHN: FORM, STYLE, SOURCES AND BACKGROUND

1. Literary Form

THE LITERARY FORM of 1 John is an enigma. The Church Fathers refer to it a 'letter', as do modern translations. But it lacks opening address, final greetings, and other marks of a letter such as personal references. Some scholars have tried to get round this by suggesting that it is a *literary* letter. But even literary letters and religious or philosophical treatises in epistolary form contain greetings (cf. Epicurus's *Letter to Menoeceus*; the *Letter of Aristeas*; the gnostic *Treatise on the Resurrection*).

F.O. Francis, in a much cited article, defended the epistolary character of 1 John, observing that not all papyrus letters have closing greetings. He claimed a parallel to 1 John's opening in a letter cited in Josephus (*Ant.* 11.123-24) and noted 1 John's reference to prayer (5.14-17), arguing that prayer is 'an established element in the epistolary close in the NT epistles'. But his arguments are unconvincing. The supposed parallel in Josephus to the 'double opening statement' of 1 Jn 1.1-3 is weak, and in any case the Josephus also contains the traditional epistolary greeting with *chairein*. 1 John does not *end* with prayer, but restates old themes in new language, finishing with a warning against idols. Moreover, there are big differences between the idiosyncratic material on prayer in 1 John and the closing Pauline benedictions cited as parallels. More recently F. Vouga (1990) has defended 1 John's status as a letter, but his theory likewise is founded on the absence of opening greetings and epistolary ending (not obviated by calling 5.13 a 'final benediction').

So what are the alternatives? Dodd and others have suggested that 1 John might be a circular letter, intended for a number of local churches. But once again the absence of greetings provides a major obstacle. If 1 John were intended for several congregations, one would expect this to be made explicit (cf. Col. 4.16; Rev. 1.4-3.1). Others see 1 John as a tract addressed to the Church at large (so Houlden). This would be compatible with the author's address to his recipients as 'beloved', 'brothers' and 'little children'—terms used by an established teacher to those viewed as pupils. The problem here is that 1 John refers to a specific doctrinal crisis and even to specific (unnamed) individuals. The difficulties are compounded by the fact that those who designate 1 John a 'tract' use the term in a bewildering range of senses. Some appear to regard it as a kind of general 'manifesto', suitable for all Christians (so Kümmel 1975: 437); others see it as denoting a homily or pastoral address to a specific audience (so Marshall). Smalley describes 1 John as a 'paper' in the modern sense, thus leaving the ancient genre unsolved. Deissmann and Dibelius both identified 1 John as a 'diatribe' (a form of ethical discourse especially favoured by Cynics and Stoics). Though it lacks the biting wit of some diatribes, it shows affinities with the more gentle paraenesis of the philosopher Epictetus. Grayston has suggested that 1 John is an *Encheiridion*, that is, an instruction book for disciples for applying a master's teaching. These proposals will be considered later.

The problem of genre is not unique to 1 John in the New Testament. The letter of James also lacks an epistolary ending, and it too has been identified as a 'diatribe' or paraenesis. Hebrews has valedictory greetings, but like 1 John no opening greetings. Possibly an original epistolary greeting for 1 John has been lost, or rather replaced by the formal prooemium. Conceivably some final greetings have also been removed when an original letter was adapted for a wider purpose. Before reaching any conclusions on form we need to look in more detail at 1 John's structure and style.

2. The Structure of 1 John

It is difficult to discern a logical structure in 1 John. Writing in 1912, Brooke went so far as to say that any attempt to analyse the Epistle should be abandoned as useless (1912: xxxii). This has not prevented numerous scholars seeking to discover an overarching plan. Schnackenburg (p. 12) proposes alternating ethical and christological themes, culminating in the tying of the two together in 4.7–5.12; but he recognizes that this does not solve all the problems. Brown (1982: 764) tabulates 42 sample attempts, dividing the text into two, three or seven parts (the most favoured divisions) plus the Prooemium and, in some cases, an Appendix. Vouga (1990) offers a fresh analysis based on ancient rhetorical and epistolary theory, but his study forces the text unnaturally into classical patterns and some of his subdivisions are quite unconvincing (e.g. the idea that the whole of 1.5–2.17 is a *captatio benevolentiae*).

The following analysis is offered as guide to aid the reader, without any claim that it represents the author's intention:

A. PROOEMIUM or formal opening (1.1-4)
B. MAIN BODY
    1. Theme of light and darkness: walking in the light as a sign of fellowship with God (1.5–2.11).
    2. Admonitions and warning against love of the world (2.12-17).
    3. The 'last hour' and true confession or denial of Christ (2.18-27)
    4. The children of God and the children of the devil (2.28–3.24)
    5. The two kinds of Spirits (4.1-6)
    6. The nature and the demands of love (4.7-21)
    7. Victory and testimony (5.1-12)
C. CONCLUSION: purpose of writing, postscripts and re-affirmations (5.13-21).

In fact, all the sections overlap in content with others. 1 John's structure has aptly been described as spiraliform: it moves from one subject to another by association of ideas, and then returns to a subject already discussed. Thus the author's thoughts on any particular subject, such as love, or sin, or spiritual birth, are not grouped systematically, but have to be culled from different parts of the writing. One is tempted to compare 1 John to a rather rambling sermon, but the writer does have a definite persuasive purpose in mind and seems to have composed in this way because he believed it was likely to gain conviction.

3. The Greek Style of 1 John

Houlden writes (p. 3): 'The impression the writer of 1J gives is of tenacious and inflexible insistence on a small number of points which he hammers again and again'. 1 John is certainly noted for its distinctive style with a limited vocabulary and a small range of grammatical constructions, which are used repeatedly. Many of these features are apparent even in translation, and we cite a few striking examples. The author is fond of 'if-clauses' where the second part of the sentence is not the logical outcome of the first, for example, 'If we accept human testimony, God's testimony is greater' (5.9), where the author means, 'If we accept human testimony, much more ought we to accept God's, since it is superior'. He loves general statements of the type, 'Anyone who does x is...' (e.g. 2.4). He makes much use of antitheses: contrasts are continually drawn between those who love their 'brothers' and those who hate them; those who 'do' the truth and those who do not. He likes using demonstratives to look forward to what he is about to say: 'And this is the message which we have heard...' (1.5, etc; cf. 2 Jn 6), or to look back: 'And this is the spirit of the antichrist' (4.3). He also uses demonstratives to give a 'test formula': 'By this we know...' (e.g. 3.19). Rather confusingly, this 'test formula' can refer either to what has preceded or to what follows (e.g. 2.3 and 2.5); sometimes it is ambiguous. The author favours short sentences and parataxis, rather than involved periods with subordinate clauses (the Prooemium is an exception). A characteristic feature of 1 John is its limited range of conjunctions or linking particles, with excessive use of 'and'.

This last feature may be due to a semitic background, since in Hebrew the conjunction 'and' serves a great variety of functions. Other possible semitic features are the use of 'everyone...not' for 'nobody'; hanging nouns, pronouns and participles, and the partitive use of 'out of', for example, 4.13, lit. 'he has given us out of his Spirit', when he means 'he has given us (a share of) his Spirit'. We may also mention the phrases 'doing the truth' (1.6), 'believing in the Name' (3.23), and 'shutting up one's bowels' in the sense of refusing to have compassion (3.17).

But some recent scholars have suggested that all three Johannines are constructed according to the elaborate rules of Graeco-Roman rhetoric. Thus Watson has argued that 1 John's repetitions are deliberately designed to make his message more effective. Far from being boring, 'the highly repetitive and emphatic nature of 1 John is one of its striking, yet unappreciated features' (1993: 99). He offers as an example 1 Jn 2.12-14—a strange passage consisting of six solemn admonitions addressed in turn to 'children', 'fathers', and 'young men'. Each group is addressed twice, with a change of tense in the verb. Scholars have puzzled whether these are people of different age-groups or different stages of Christian development, or whether, by a kind of poetic licence, they might be addressed to all believers as they develop in maturity in their Christian life. Some commentators have even suggested that we have two drafts of the same material.

Watson (1989) proposes that this is an example of the rhetorical figures of *distributio, conduplicatio* and *expolitio* ('distribution', 'reduplication', 'polishing'). In v. 12 the author addresses the whole group as 'children'; next he addresses two sub-groups, 'fathers' and 'young men' (*distributio*). Then he repeats his admonitions with an elegant variation in the word for 'children' and a change of tense (*conduplicatio*). He also varies his reasons for addressing the groups (*expolitio*). The whole passage, Watson claims, is formally a *digressio* (digression), which serves an emotional function in praising the audience and creating goodwill after the author's initial establishment of his premises and refutation of opponents. But similar repetitions occur regularly in the Hebrew Bible (e.g. Ps. 148.12), and one wonders whether much is gained by offering such sophisticated names to this obscure passage. Classical rhetoric hardly seems to be the key to 1 John's style.

4. Written or Oral Sources?

Other scholars have sought to explain 1 John's peculiar structure and syntax by theories of sources. In 1907 E. von Dobschütz isolated four pairs of antithetical statements in 1 Jn 2.28–3.12 which he suggested were derived from a Hellenistic source which had been expanded with hortatory material. Bultmann went further. In a long article in the *Festgabe für A. Jülicher* (1927) he identified 26 antithetical pairs (or triplets), which he believed came from a 'gnostic' environment. Bultmann, like Dobschütz, argued that the main source (*Vorlage* or *Grundschrift*) has been split up by the author of 1 John and interspersed with homiletic or hortatory material. Bultmann's theory has been strongly criticized by Brown. Apart from questions over the proposed gnostic background, the chief problem is why, if the author had a coherent source before him, did he break it up so unsatisfactorily and scatter the antithetical sayings? Similar problems arise with the theory of W. Nauck, who in *Die Tradition und der Charakter des ersten Johannesbriefes* (1957) argued that the postulated 'source' was composed by the author of 1 John himself. But who would mutilate their own work in this way? There are also many uncertainties as to what was in the original *Vorlage*, and what is redaction.

In 1966 J.C. O'Neill argued that 1 John incorporates twelve poetic admonitions from a Jewish source. But this postulated source is too hypothetical to win credence, and, besides some odd interpretations, the theory involves excising phrases to provide the poetic structures. Both Nauck and O'Neill have done a service in highlighting 1 John's *Jewish* background. They had the advantage, not available to Dobschütz and Bultmann (in his original article), of the newly published Dead Sea Scrolls with all that they have to contribute to our understanding of first-century Judaism.

If the specific source theories of these authors have not won many adherents, the distinctions they made between different kinds of material in 1 John have been widely accepted. Two main types have been identified: (a) didactic or apodeictic, that is, quasi-credal statements of common belief, and (b) hortatory or homiletic material. But sometimes the author seems to shift from one type of statement to the other, and it is not always clear to which category some sentences belong. Grayston therefore suggests that 1 John has more than one author—a group of Christian leaders who composed an initial agreed statement (1.1–2.11), and a main writer who used and expanded this statement. Others see the variations in style as due to a single author's dual purpose: first, to state Christian truth and correct error; and secondly, to encourage his community (so Schnackenburg). The case for multiple authorship or specific identifiable sources has not been proved; nevertheless, it remains probable that our present text does incorporate material from a variety of sources.

In an important study O.A. Piper (1947) drew attention to the extent to which the author draws on common tradition shared between himself and his readers, for example, the love command. Terms like 'antichrist', 'chrism' and 'God's seed' are introduced without explanation, presuming that the readers are familiar with them. There are frequent references to 'what you know' or 'what you have heard from the beginning', as well as direct professions of faith (e.g. 4.2). Piper reckons that there are at least 30 passages where reference to a common faith is certain, as well as around 20 other possible examples. He argues that the author is drawing on his own oral teaching. Piper does not preclude the idea of some pre-formed material (e.g. 1.6-10 with its 'hymnic' structure), but he strongly argues that there is no *written* source; only *oral* materials lie behind the text. Similar ideas were put forward by Dodd (1946), who believed that the author is drawing on the Church's basic *kerygma* or tradition, though he cites it in a 'gnosticizing' and 'Johannine' form. The idea of an oral tradition behind 1 John, either in the author's own preaching or in the Church's *catechesis*, has much to commend it. But how far does the teaching of 1 John conform to mainstream Christian tradition? Many scholars have postulated Hellenistic-Gnostic affinities.

5. The Background of 1 John

In the 1930s Dodd suggested that Gnosticism formed an important element in the background to 1 John. He took as an example 'This is the message we heard from him, "God is light"' (1.5). The author speaks as if he is giving his audience a well-known axiom. But where in the Gospels, Dodd asks, do we find the sentiment 'God is light'? It occurs in a Hellenistic pagan writing from Egypt—the *Hermetic Corpus* (1.6) where the god Poimandres declares, 'I am that light, Nous your God' (*Nous* = Mind, Intelligence, Reason). Similar thoughts are found in Philo, a Jewish first-century writer much influenced by Greek philosophy: 'God is light...and not only light but the archetype of every other light' (*De Somn.* 1.75). The *Hermetic Corpus* lays stress on knowledge of God as the source of salvation, and on ideas of 'seeing' God mystically, of rebirth, and of being identified with God. Dodd also cited parallels to 1 John's striking use of *sperma*, 'seed', and *chrisma*, 'anointing' in Gnosticism (1937: 147-53).

The discovery of a library of Coptic gnostic texts in 1945 confirmed Dodd's hunch that the concepts of divine 'seed' and 'anointing' are thoroughly at home in Gnosticism. The *Gospel of Philip* knows 'chrism' as a 'mystery' alongside baptism and eucharist. Couched in typically obscure language the text states: 'It is from water and fire and light that the son of the bridal chamber came into being. The fire is the chrism, the light is the fire' (2.3, NHL 140). Other texts which speak of a spiritual chrism include the *Pistis Sophia* and the *Gospel of Truth*; the latter mentions also 'the light which is perfect and filled with the seed of the Father' (1.3, NHL 49). The idea of divine seed impregnating Silence, who gave birth to *Nous*, is attested as gnostic by Irenaeus in his *Refutation of Heresies* (1.1.1). It is not surprising that a number of scholars today, including most notably Vouga, see Gnosticism as an important factor in 1 John's background.

At first sight the parallels between 1 John and the Nag Hammadi texts are impressive: but when one examines the material in its fuller context, one is struck by the real differences between their theology and 1 John's. The whole thought-system presupposed by Valentinian Gnosticism is vast and complex, and quite alien to 1 John's. Nearly all the texts are later than any plausible date for 1 John: the *Pistis Sophia* and *Gospel of Truth*, for example, are probably second century CE, the *Gospel of Philip* probably later third century CE. Rather than being a source for Johannine thought, these texts were likely influenced by it. Is there any other possible source nearer to hand?

The metaphor of God as light is found already in the Hebrew Bible (e.g. Ps. 27.1; 36.9), though without 1 John's sharp light–dark dichotomy and underlying dualism. Closer parallels are provided by the Dead Sea Scrolls (first discovered in 1947). These are the writings of a Jewish group who separated themselves from their fellow-Jews to live a life of asceticism, prayer and community at Qumran, by the Dead Sea. They date from before 70 CE. The most striking parallels to 1 John cluster in the *Manual of Discipline* or *Community Rule* (1QS), which makes continual contrasts between good and evil, light and dark, truth and falsehood. This text divides humanity into two camps, the 'sons of light' and the 'sons of darkness'. God has appointed two spirits for them, the 'Spirit of Truth' and the 'Spirit of Falsehood' (or 'Perversity'). 'Those born of truth spring from a fountain of light, but those born of falsehood spring from a source of darkness. All the children of righteousness are ruled by the Prince of Light and walk in the ways of light, but all the children of falsehood are ruled by the Angel of Darkness and walk in the ways of darkness. The Angel of Darkness leads all the children of righteousness astray...' (1 QS 3; Vermes 65). One is immediately reminded of 1 John's references to the 'Spirit of Truth' and the 'Spirit of Error' (4.6), and of its dualistic framework generally. The similarities of thought are not confined to 1 John, but extend also to the Gospel of John.

In both the Qumran texts and 1 John the dualism is moral and eschatological rather than absolute, as in Zoroastrianism (where good and evil contend as equal powers). God is in control; indeed in Johannine theology victory has already been won (1 Jn 5.4; cf. Jn 16.33). Qumran dualism also differs from the dualism of developed Gnosticism in that God, not a demiurge, is creator, and creation is good.

The Qumran texts stress the unity or 'community' (Heb. *yaḥad*) of their members; we may compare the *koinōnia*), or fellowship, of 1 John. They emphasize the need for confession of sin, witness, enlightenment from God, and the cleansing work of the Spirit of Truth (1 QS 4). All these features have parallels in the Johannine corpus. The Qumran covenanters are taught to love their 'brothers' as themselves and to succour the poor, needy and strangers (CD 6; Vermes 88). 'Brothers' here means members of the community. A particularly interesting parallel concerns the Covenanters' use of the term 'idols'. Any member who 'walks among the idols of his heart, who sets up before himself his stumbling-block of sin so that he may backslide' is cursed (1 QS 2; Vermes 63). It has been plausibly suggested that the strange final warning of 1 Jn 5.21 refers not to pagan images, but to these 'idols of the heart'—sinful thoughts which lead to backsliding and ultimately apostasy.

In studying the Johannine literature and the Scrolls one observes many other similarities of language and thought; but there are also significant differences. The Qumran texts contain no parallel to 1 John's 'chrism' and 'seed', or the concept of being 'born of God'. They frequently refer to the Covenant, never explicitly mentioned in 1 John. They await a future messiah (or messiahs), whereas the Johannines affirm that the messiah has already come. The Qumran community is hierarchically organized with strict rules and penalties for misconduct, whereas the Johannine community seems informally structured. Qumran piety is centred round the Jewish Law and its correct interpretation, whereas Johannine faith focuses on Jesus as Son of God and messiah. On the other hand, we must remember that a large range of texts survive from Qumran reflecting the life of the community—rule books, hymns, prayers, florilegia and exegetical works—whereas for the community believed to lie behind 1 John we have very limited evidence.

Some scholars (e.g. F.M. Braun) have been so impressed at the parallels between Johannine and Qumran thought that they believe the Johannine writer(s) must have been directly influenced by Qumran. But most are more cautious. Brown believes that the Scrolls provide better parallels to Johannine thought than Hellenistic-Gnostic texts cited by Dodd and Bultmann, but at the same time he argues they cannot be seen as a direct source for John's thought (in Charlesworth 1972: 7).

We may sum up by saying that the Scrolls illuminate a

Palestinian-Jewish background to 1 John, but they form only part of its milieu. 1 John clearly owes much to the Hebrew Bible, and there are also parallels in Gnosticism and extra-biblical Jewish literature. *The Testaments of the Twelve Patriarchs* have an ethical earnestness strongly reminiscent of 1 John: they stress the importance of love (e.g. *T. Benj.* 3). They too speak of the Spirit of Truth and the Spirit of Error, and the forensic role of the former (*T. Jud.* 20). But there are problems in using these texts as a source for Johannine thought because of possible Christian editing. The Qumran texts by contrast not only predate the Johannines but are also free from Christian interference. Thus they are especially significant. The Johannine writings are not unique in the New Testament in showing affinities with Qumran thought: light-darkness dualism is found in other New Testament texts (e.g. Ephesians).

This leads us to an important point. We have so far concentrated on potential backgrounds in Jewish and Hellenistic-Gnostic thought, but we should never forget the Johannines' debt to basic Christian tradition. Dodd himself drew attention to phrases and ideas which 1 John shares with the *kerygma* of the Synoptic Gospels, especially Matthew (1946: xxxviii-xxxix). More significant, perhaps, is the possible debt of 1 John to the Gospel of John (discussed further in Chapter 4 §4). The interesting question of the relation of 1 John's thought to that of the remaining New Testament writings (e.g. Paul, James, 1 Peter) is rarely touched on, though we shall return to it in Chapter 9 (esp. §§2-3).

6. Conclusions

1 John has a loose structure and a distinctive style. It is not a letter in the normal sense of the term, and its designation as such by the Church Fathers may be because there was no other clear category in which to place it. Nor is it a 'tract', in the sense that the writings of the Hermetic Corpus or the Nag Hammadi Library are tracts. It contains homiletic material, but is clearly more than a written sermon. In its hortatory sections, it shows affinities with Testamentary literature, but it is neither a 'testament' nor a philosophical

treatise masquerading as a letter. It has striking parallels in the Qumran *Manual of Discipline*, but is less legal and prescriptive than this rule-book. Nevertheless, it may have been designed for use in a particular Christian community.

Suggestions for written sources (Bultmann, Nauck, O'Neill) have not proved convincing. The memorable, rhythmic, antithetical style and frequent repetitions suggest the inclusion of material designed for oral delivery and perhaps memorization. An intriguing hypothesis is that of Grayston that it might have been intended as an *Encheiridion* or handbook. Ancient examples of this genre (not discussed by Grayston) are Epictetus's *Encheiridion*, summarizing the ethical teaching of his *Diatribes* or *Discourses* (which also survive) and Augustine's *Enchiridion*, which he made himself as a summary of his teaching. If 1 John were a summary of the oral teaching of a great master, perhaps originally a native semitic speaker, this could explain its hortatory tone, its loose structure and ambiguities, its repetitions and even its occasional references to a specific situation (retained because of their wider applicability). However, we have to ask how widely known in the Jewish world was the specific genre of the *Encheiridion*? Whatever its literary form, 1 John is geared to the needs of readers who share the author's basic religious presuppositions and commitment. Its primary purpose seems to be to keep them on the right course in their journey of faith.

Further Reading

Genre, Structure and Style:
Brown 1982.
Dodd 1937, 1946.
F.O. Francis, 'The Form and Function of the Opening and Closing Paragraphs of James and 1 John', *ZNW* 61 (1970), pp. 110-26.
Grayston.
Houlden.
Kümmel 1975.
Schnackenburg.
Vouga in Kaestli 1990: 285-88.

Rhetorical Analyses:

H.-J. Klauck, 'Zur rhetorischen Analyse der Johannesbriefe', *ZNW* 81 (1990), pp. 205-24.

Vouga in Kaestli.

D.F. Watson, '1 John 2.12-14 as *Distributio, Conduplicatio*, and *Expolitio*: A Rhetorical Understanding', *JSNT* 35 (1989), pp. 97-110.

—'Amplification Techniques in 1 John: The Interaction of Rhetorical Style and Invention', *JSNT* 51 (1993), pp. 99-123.

Sources:

Brown 1982: 760-61 (for Bultmann's reconstructed source).

R. Bultmann, 'Analyse des ersten Johannesbriefes', in *Festgabe für Adolf Jülicher* (Tübingen, 1927), pp. 138-58.

E. von Dobschütz, 'Johanneische Studien I', *ZNW* 8 (1907), pp. 1-8.

Marshall 1978: 30 (on Nauck).

O.A. Piper, 'I John and the Didache of the Primitive Church', *JBL* 66 (1947), pp. 437-51.

J.C. O'Neill, *The Puzzle of 1 John* (London: SPCK, 1966).

Background:

J.H. Charlesworth 1972

—*The Old Testament Pseudepigrapha*. I (London: Darton, Longman & Todd, 1983) (for *Testaments of the Twelve Patriarchs*).

C.H. Dodd, 'The First Epistle of John and the Fourth Gospel', *BJRL* 21 (1937), pp. 129-56.

J.M. Robinson (ed.), *The Nag Hammadi Library* (San Francisco: Harper & Row, 1977).

K. Stendahl (ed.), *The Scrolls and the New Testament* (London: SCM Press, 1958), esp. ch. 12.

G. Vermes, *The Dead Sea Scrolls in English* (Harmondsworth: Penguin, rev. edn, 1987).

F. Vouga, 'The Johannine School: A Gnostic Tradition in Primitive Christianity?', *Bib* 69 (1988), pp. 371-85.

Relation to the Gospel of John:

Brooke 1912: i-xxvii (with much citation in Greek).

Brown 1982: 32-35 with Chart II, pp. 757-59.

Grayston 1984: 12-14.

Schnackenburg: 32-39.

4

WHO WROTE THE
JOHANNINES AND WHEN?

1. Patristic Evidence

THE QUESTION 'WHO WROTE THE JOHANNINES?' cannot be separated from that of the authorship of the Gospel of John and Revelation. From the fourth century CE all these writings were ascribed in the manuscripts to 'John'. The fact that no further identification is given suggests that the most famous New Testament John is intended, namely John, the son of Zebedee. It is likely that these titles are older than their first attestation; indeed there are hints that the chief 'Johannine' writings were attributed to the Apostle as early as c. 200 CE.

The evidence is complex, and for the views of some early witnesses we have to depend on summaries in later sources, which may not be reliable. The situation is complicated by the fact that John is a common name, and even when 'John' is further defined as 'the disciple of the Lord', one still cannot be sure that the Apostle is intended. Moreover, legend-making was rife in the early patristic period, as can be seen from the various apocryphal Acts, and there was a strong desire to attribute as many writings as possible to apostolic figures. With these cautions in mind we review the patristic evidence.

An early witness is Irenaeus of Lyons (died c. 200), who more than once refers to 'John, the Lord's disciple', who 'reclined on his breast', whom he takes to be the author of the Gospel of John, Revelation, and 1 John. He may not have been the first to do so: the Gnostic Ptolemaeus, whom

Irenaeus quotes, ascribed at least the Gospel Prologue to 'John', and the orthodox father Theophilus of Antioch (? c. 180) quotes from the Gospel of John as by 'John' (though he does not identify him as an apostle). Irenaeus clearly attests developed traditions about this John: he believed that he wrote his Gospel after the other three in his old age, and he associates it with Ephesus where, he says, John lived into the reign of Trajan (98–117). Irenaeus also quotes from what we now call 1 and 2 John, but he treats these as a single letter.

Another important witness is the Muratorian Canon. This list of New Testament writings is generally believed to have been composed at Rome c. 190–200 (though some favour an Eastern origin and a fourth-century date). This ascribes the Gospel, *two* Epistles and the Apocalypse to 'John', and quotes the opening of 1 John in defence of the Gospel of John, assuming its author to be an eye-witness. This text seems to be reacting against doubts concerning the orthodoxy of the Gospel of John, possibly because it was so much used by Gnostics. Clement of Alexandria (c. 150–215) quotes from the 'greater Epistle of John' (presumably 1 John), and Tertullian (c. 160–225) ascribes 1 John, the Gospel and the Apocalypse to the Apostle John. Other writers from the third to fifth centuries echo similar views.

Based on this patristic evidence a seemingly attractive hypothesis has been put forward that John, the son of Zebedee—one of Jesus' original twelve apostles—in later life migrated from Palestine to Ephesus, had a spell of exile on Patmos (where he wrote the Apocalypse), returning to Ephesus, where he composed the Gospel and 1–3 John. Polycrates, bishop of Ephesus (c. 189–98) says that 'John' died at Ephesus; his tomb was shown there in antiquity (Culpepper 1994: chs. 4–6; Brown 1966; 1982).

But will this hypothesis stand up to close examination? The New Testament gives no hint that the Apostle John ever went to Ephesus. Mk 10.39 predicts the martyrdom of the two sons of Zebedee: James, we know, was martyred early and there was a tradition (incompatible with Irenaeus's testimony) that John also died young (see Barrett 1978: 103, citing Papias and other authorities). Moreover, only Revelation out of all the New Testament 'Johannine' writings actually claims to be by someone called John, and even this gives no hint that its author was an Apostle. It has been strongly argued (Gunther 1980) that its author was an Asian prophet, who erroneously got identified, first with John the son of Zebedee, and later with the author of the Gospel of John and the Johannine Epistles. The Gospel of John and 1 John are both strictly anonymous; 2–3 John's claim to be written by a 'presbyter' will be discussed later.

Sometimes it is alleged that Irenaeus's testimony is of great value since in his youth he lived in Asia Minor and knew Polycarp, bishop of Smyrna, who reputedly knew John the Apostle. But it must be noted that Polycarp himself never attributes the authorship of the Gospel of John or 1–3 John to the son of Zebedee. Ignatius (who wrote to the Ephesians and other Churches in Asia) is also silent on this, and says nothing about any connection between John and Ephesus.

The status of 2 and 3 John is especially doubtful. These letters were omitted from the Syriac text of the New Testament until the fifth to sixth centuries, which strongly suggests that apostolic authorship was not attributed to them. None of the writers we have earlier cited mentions 3 John, and some refer to just one letter by John. The great biblical scholar Origen (c. 185–254) doubted the authenticity of 2 and 3 John. Eusebius admits that their canonicity was disputed. Although Jerome (c. 342–420) himself believed that all three Johannine letters were by the Apostle, he too attests the belief that 2 and 3 John were by a different author, whom he calls 'John the Presbyter'. The idea of two men called John, both living at Ephesus, is found in a number of other authors (Lieu 1986: ch. 1), and some scholars have conjectured that the Epistles and Gospel were written by this second John (cf. Hengel; Bauckham). Others, however, dispute his very existence.

All this suggests that the patristic testimony concerning 'apostolic' authorship of 1–3 John should be regarded with reservation, and that we must take also careful account of the internal evidence.

2. Internal Evidence

2 and 3 John claim to be written by a presbyter or 'elder', a
term probably denoting ecclesiastical office. It is unlikely an
apostle would so designate himself, especially if he were
seeking to assert his authority in matters of hospitality or
doctrine. This means that if 1 John is by the same author as
2–3 John, it is unlikely to be by an apostle. Recently, however, the common authorship of 1–3 John has been strongly
challenged. Several eminent scholars believe that 2–3 John
were written by a different author from 1 John, and some
even separate the authorship of the two shorter letters. A
good case has been made for regarding 2 John as dependent
on both 1 John and 3 John, but this is compatible with either
common authorship for 2–3 John (so Grayston) or separate
authorship (so Bultmann). In neither case do we get much
help over the authorship of 1 John. The canonical history of
the letters sheds little light on the problem, except to show
that 2 and 3 John are not a 'pair of inseparable twins' (the
phrase is Judith Lieu's).

The presence of semitic turns of expression in all three
Johannines points to an author of Jewish origin. This would
be compatible with authorship by John the Apostle, but does
not demand it. It has sometimes been argued that the apparent claim to eye-witness in 1 Jn 1.1-4 points to apostolic
authorship. But there were other eye-witnesses besides the
son of Zebedee! In any case, in spite of the emphatic verbs of
perception, these verses are more plausibly read as a claim to
continuity with apostolic tradition (cf. Loader: 4). The case
for John the son of Zebedee as the author of 1 John has to
rest on a threefold identification: (a) the epistolary writer(s)
with the author of John's Gospel; (b) the Gospel author with
the 'beloved disciple'; (c) the 'beloved disciple' with the son of
Zebedee—all assumptions which must be discussed.

3. 1 John and the Gospel of John

Was 1 John written by the same person as the Gospel of
John? The style and thought of the two writings are so similar that numerous scholars have argued that the same man

must have composed both (see Guthrie 1970: 876-81; Marshall 1978; 1982: 1096-97). Yet as early as the nineteenth century H.J. Holzmann pointed out differences in both theology and style. His arguments were taken up and amplified by Dodd. In spite of various attempts (e.g. by Brooke, Howard and Wilson) to demonstrate a single mind behind these two texts, the idea of separate authorship has grown in popularity, and is today favoured by such scholars as Grayston, Houlden, Lieu and, more hesitatingly, Schnackenburg. The evidence is highly complex. On the one hand 1 John and the Gospel have a large stock of similar vocabulary and turns of expression, and a common fund of distinctive theological ideas. On the other hand, there are subtle differences of style (e.g. in the use of particles, prepositions and participles). There are also different nuances in theology (e.g. over the atonement, parousia, Spirit). One problem in reaching a conclusion is knowing how much allowance to make for possible variations within the style of a single author and for developments of thought in response to a fresh situation. Also John's Gospel and 1 John belong to different genres, the gospel-form being essentially narrative and epistles hortatory.

This last difference is not so great as one might suppose, since John's Gospel contains much theological discourse similar in style to the hortatory material of 1 John. In fact, one of the most interesting stylistic observations that have been made is that 1 John stands especially close to the more reflective parts of the Gospel of John, notably John 13–17. This raises a fresh question. Is the Gospel itself a literary unity? Numerous scholars have pointed out *aporiae* or awkward transitions suggesting seams between traditions or, possibly, different sources. It is widely believed that the Fourth Gospel had a long literary development, and went through more than one edition (so Barrett, Brown, Schnackenburg). Chapters 13–17 are among the material frequently attributed to the Gospel's (hypothetical) second edition. Could it be that the author of 1 John was a reviser or editor of the Gospel? Such a hypothesis is difficult either to prove or to refute.

We now turn to the enigma of the 'beloved disciple'. This

figure appears only in the Gospel of John's passion and re-surrection narrative (13.23; 19.26-27; 20.2-10; 21.7, 20-23). He is portrayed as specially close to Jesus, being present at the Last Supper and the crucifixion. Chapter 21 (probably an appendix) appears to identify him as author: 'This is the dis-ciple who is bearing witness to these things, and who has written these things; and we know that his witness is true' (21.24). While some scholars suppose that 'these things' refers only to the resurrection appearance just described, it is much more plausible that the phrase is intended to denote the whole Gospel. In other words the author(s) of Jn 21.24 are promoting 'the disciple whom Jesus loved' as the autho-rity behind John's Gospel. He is its 'ideal' author (so Bauckham).

But who wrote this verse? The use of the first person plur-al suggests a group. It has been plausibly suggested that it alludes to a Johannine school, circle or community, gathered round their leader the 'beloved disciple' (so Culpepper, Cullmann, Brown). 'School', 'circle' and 'community' are not exact synonyms: 'school' implies a more formal structure like an ancient philosophical school, 'circle' a more loosely orga-nized group, and 'community' a body of people sharing a com-mon social and religious life. John's Gospel never reveals the identity of this 'beloved disciple'. He appears to be one of the seven fishermen listed in Jn 21.2; he *could* have been one of the sons of Zebedee mentioned there, but he could equally have been one of the unnamed disciples. Some identify him with the Apostle John; some with the 'Elder' John (Hengel supposes that he reflects both at once). Others have argued that he must be regarded as strictly anonymous—an other-wise unknown early Christian leader (so Cullmann). Bultmann saw him as a purely ideal figure. While dogma-tism is out of place, the most likely conclusion is that he was a real person known to those in his own circle, who played a significant role in putting the Gospel into its present form. The internal evidence is insufficient to substantiate the patristic identification of him with either John, the son of Zebedee, or the shadowy 'John the Elder'. Whether or not this figure is identical with the author(s) of 1–3 John is doubtful. The idea of a Johannine community with a distinctive theology and style, and more than one theological writer, remains the best explanation of both the similarities and dissimilarities of the Johannine corpus.

4. The Date of the Johannines

Any attempt to date 1–3 John is fraught with difficulty because of the lack of objective criteria. There are no allusions to datable events (e.g. the accession of a Roman emperor), or to datable individuals. None of the persons named—Gaius, Demetrius, Diotrephes—is known from other sources (the first two are very common names in the Roman Empire, and attempts to identify them with other New Testament figures of the same name have been unsuccessful). Nor are allusions to Church order much help in dating. If Diotrephes (or the Elder) were an emerging monarchic bishop, then this might point to a date late in the first century, contemporary with *1 Clement* and possibly the Pastoral Epistles, or even as late as Ignatius (c. 110–140), that great enthusiast for the episcopate! But, as was seen in Chapter 2, a much more informal Church order seems likely. Even this does not help much, since informal patterns seem to have continued alongside more structured ministries for many years. References to travelling missionaries occur in such chronologically diverse contexts as Paul's genuine letters, the Gospels of Matthew and Luke and the *Didache* (? c. 90–120).

It might be supposed that the references to false teachers could aid dating. But scholars are unable to reach agreement on the identity of the opponents, opinions varying between Jews, Cerinthians, Docetists and Gnostics (cf. below, Chapter 5). Even if one of these groups could be securely identified as the 'opponents', a wide range of dates would still be possible.

The securest evidence for dating 1 John comes from external sources, notably citations in patristic writings. According to Eusebius the 'former Epistle of John' was used by Papias (? c. 130 CE). There are a number of possible echoes in Ignatius, Barnabas, Justin Martyr, Hermas and the *Epistle to Diognetus* (all probably second century CE). It is not certain whether 1 John was known to Polycarp (early second century). In *Phil.* 7.1, in language very similar to 1 Jn 4.2-3 and 2 Jn 7, he writes: 'Everyone who does not confess that Jesus Christ has come in the flesh is an Antichrist; and whoever does not confess the witness of the cross is of the devil'. While some scholars have argued that he is drawing on a common stock of vocabulary and ideas, it seems more probable that these words are dependent on 1 or 2 John (or both). All this suggests that 1 John was known in patristic circles in the *first half* of the second century. Earlier than this we cannot go with any confidence, since the alleged echoes in *1 Clement* are too doubtful to be of any use. The patristic citations, of course, provide only an *ante quem*: the Johannines might have been newly written when cited, or much older.

Could it be that 1–3 John were actually written before the Gospel of John? It has been argued that they present a more primitive *Christology*: for example, Jn 1.14 boldly identifies Jesus with the Logos, whereas 1 Jn 1.1 speaks more indirectly of 'the word of life'—and does so ambiguously, so that one cannot tell whether it is talking about Jesus personally or the gospel message. The Epistles, it has been argued, also presuppose a more primitive *soteriology*: they speak crudely of the blood of Jesus washing away sin (1 Jn 1.7), whereas the Gospel uses more subtle imagery (cf. Jn 19.34). 1 John expects an imminent *parousia* (e.g. 2.18), while the Gospel works mostly with a sophisticated 'realized' eschatology. 1 John seems to refer to the Spirit impersonally as an 'unction' (2.27), whereas the Gospel (or at least Jn 14–16) has a more developed doctrine of a personal Holy Spirit. All this evidence could point to a chronological priority of 1 John, as has been eloquently argued by Grayston.

On the other hand theological simplicity does not necessarily mean chronological priority. The evidence is also consistent with the view that these Epistles represent a rearguard action by a conservative Christian, who has been distressed at the way some 'progressive' thinkers have taken certain Johannine concepts to extremes. His references to those who do not accept Jesus as the 'Christ come in the flesh' have been taken as polemic against 'docetic' thinkers who had concluded from the Gospel's affirmation of Jesus' divinity that he was not truly human. Similarly, the allusion to Jesus' blood washing away sin could be seen as a response to those who thought of his death merely as an example. But 1 John's Christology is by no means 'low': Jesus and the Father are frequently treated on an equal footing, and in many sentences it is ambiguous to which of these the author refers; at least one text may attribute divinity to Jesus (5.20). 1 John also contains several passages which *may* echo the Gospel, notably 2.7; 3.14 and 3.15 (cf. Jn 13.34; 5.24; 8.44). All this is consistent with the view that 1 John was written *after* the Gospel of John, as has been argued by many recent scholars, including Houlden, Brown, Marshall and Smalley.

While no certainty is possible, the balance of the evidence favours the idea that 1 John was written after at least a first edition of the Gospel of John (so Schnackenburg). But one cannot preclude that parts of the Gospel (e.g. the Prologue and ch. 21) were composed after 1 John was written. With that we shall have to be content. It should also be noted that the dating of the Gospel is itself controversial. While some scholars have supported an early date, most experts favour one late in the first century, after the split between Christianity and Judaism (c. 85–100 CE). The idea that 1 John was written to *accompany* the Gospel or as an explicit refutation of misunderstandings of it seems unlikely in view of the shortage of clear citations from it.

As for 2–3 John, the evidence is even more scanty. Some see the reference to a previous letter in 3 Jn 10 as an allusion to 2 John; more probably it refers to a lost letter. The fact that 3 John is written in a very simple style does not mean that it *must* be early. It seems plausible on literary grounds that 2 John is dependent on 3 John, but we have to admit no certainty is possible.

5. Conclusions

The results of this investigation have proved rather meagre. We do not know *who* wrote 1–3 John nor *when* they were written, nor even *in what order* they were written. It is still possible to argue for a common authorship of 1–3 John and the Gospel of John by John, the son of Zebedee, though this now seems unlikely. Little is gained from postulating Papias's 'Elder' John as author. 1 John might have been written before or after the Gospel, or between two editions of the Gospel, though a date after its main composition seems most likely. A plausible order for the Epistles is 3 John, 1 John, 2 John, but alternatives are possible. 1–3 John might be by one, two, or even three different authors. As for an absolute date, the Gospel and at least 1–2 John seem to be known to patristic writers by the second century CE; a date towards the end of the first century seems quite plausible. Whatever the chronology, the Gospel and all three Epistles are clearly related. The hypothesis of a Johannine 'school' or 'community' centred round the 'beloved disciple' has much to commend it.

Further Reading

Introductions to commentaries on 1–3 John by Brooke; Brown; Grayston; Houlden; Loader; Marshall; Schnackenburg; also to commentaries on the Gospel of John by Barrett (1978) and Brown (1966). Also see Brown 1979.

R. Bauckham, 'The Beloved Disciple as Ideal Author', *JSNT* 49 (1993), pp. 21-44.

O. Cullmann, *The Johannine Circle* (ET; London: SCM Press, 1976).

R.A. Culpepper, *The Johannine School* (Missoula, MT: Scholars Press, 1975).

—*John, the Son of Zebedee* (Columbia: University of South Carolina Press, 1994).

J.J. Gunther, 'Early Identifications of the Authorship of the Johannine Writings', *JEH* 31 (1980), pp. 407-27.

D. Guthrie, *New Testament Introduction* (London: Inter-Varsity Press, rev. edn, 1970).

M. Hengel, *The Johannine Question* (ET; London: SCM Press; Philadelphia: Trinity Press International, 1989).

J. Lieu, *The Second and Third Epistles of John* (Edinburgh: T. & T. Clark, 1986).

On Style and Language:

C.H. Dodd, 'The First Epistle of John and the Fourth Gospel', *BJRL* 21 (1937), pp. 129-56.

W.F. Howard, 'The Common Authorship of the Johannine Gospel and Epistles', *JTS* 48 (1947), pp. 12-25.

W.G. Wilson, 'An Examination of the Linguistic Evidence Adduced against the Unity of Authorship of the First Epistle of John and the Fourth Gospel', *JTS* 49 (1948), pp. 147-56.

5

CHRISTOLOGY AND
THE 'OPPONENTS'

1. Introduction

1 JOHN WAS ESPECIALLY valued in antiquity for its 'orthodox' Christology. Yet curiously it contains no systematic exposition of doctrine: doctrinal beliefs are assumed rather than argued. The author deals with them as they arise, in no discernible order, but as suits his rhetorical purpose. Many scholars have seen this purpose as polemical—to attack false teachers or dissidents. R.A. Whitacre (1982) sees 1 John as continuing, at a different level, a polemical stance found already in the Gospel. P. Bonnard goes so far as to call all three Johannines 'fundamentally polemical from beginning to end' (1983: 14). Numerous attempts have been made to identify the 'opponents' in question: charismatics, Jews, Cerinthians, Docetists, and Gnostics have all been suggested. Scholars have assiduously sought to delineate their errant ethics and Christology by careful analysis of the text; some have postulated more than one group of adversaries. Elaborate hypotheses have been put forward about the history of the Johannine community and the fate of the various groups. The present chapter challenges the view that the primary purpose of the Johannines was polemical, and seeks a more positive understanding of their Christology.

2. Methodology

In the search for 'opponents' interest has naturally centred on 1 John, the longest of the three Epistles, with the fullest ethical and christological content. Attention has already been drawn (above Chapter 3 §3) to the author's fondness for certain kinds of conditional ('if') clauses and general statements of the type, 'anyone who does x is y'. These have regularly been interpreted as polemical in character. Thus when the author writes, 'If we say that we have fellowship with him and walk in the darkness we are liars' (1.6), it is assumed he is 'getting at' a group who claim a special fellowship with God. Similarly the statements, 'The one who says "I know him" and does not keep his commandments is a liar' (2.4), and 'Nobody who remains in him sins' (3.6) and 'Everyone who hates his "brother" is a murderer' (3.15), are taken to refer to these adversaries who claim to 'know' God and be sinless, while blatantly breaking God's law and hating their fellow-Christians. The fullest reconstructions of opponents' views made on these lines are by Brown (1982: 762-63) and Painter (1986).

The problem with the method is that it fails to allow sufficiently for the author's vigorous and and idiosyncratic 'upfront' style. He loves antithesis: 'If we say that we have no sin, we deceive ourselves and the truth is not in us. If we confess our sins, he is faithful and just to forgive us our sins and cleanse us from all unrighteousness' (1.8-9). Those who see this as polemic fail to take the 'we' seriously. Rather than attacking a specific group of 'opponents' who claim to be sinless, the author is warning his own community that they must not make this claim. Moreover, it is usually assumed that 1 John's distinctive vocabulary is drawn from the 'opponents', notably such terms as *koinōnia*, 'fellowship', *chrisma*, 'unction' and *sperma*, 'seed' (of God). Hence Painter suggests that the 'opponents' are perfectionist charismatics, who claim a special fellowship with God and a divine anointing which preserves them from sin. It is true that the words 'fellowship' and 'unction' are not found in the Gospel of John, nor is 'seed' with reference to God, but there is no reason why, if 1 John is by a different author, he should not use different vocabulary; even if the two texts are by the same man, not enough of his writing survives to enable us with confidence to say that certain vocabulary *must* have come from an outside source. The author nowhere attributes to *opponents* claims to have 'community' or spiritual 'anointing'; rather he reassures his readers that this is what they themselves have (cf. 1.3; 2.20, 26). The idea that 1 John, in its ethical teaching, is attacking a group of charismatic 'pneumatics' who profess to be sinless is ill-founded. It is the author's own community for whom he claims special guidance from the Holy Spirit (cf. Jn 16.13).

3. Christological Confessions and Controversies

What of our author's christological statements? These first appear in 1 Jn 2.18-25, when he announces that it is the 'last hour' and adduces as evidence that the expected 'Antichrist' has come in those who deny Christ. He writes: 'Who is the liar but the one denying that Jesus is the Christ? This is the Antichrist, the one denying the Father and the Son' (2.22). It is clear from the context that he is speaking of a specific group of Johannine Christians who have seceded from the community who, he claims, never really belonged to it (2.19). 2 John also seems to refer to specific opponents when it says, 'Many deceivers have gone out into the world, who do not confess Jesus Christ coming in the flesh. This is the deceiver and the Antichrist' (v. 7). It is unclear whether these are the same group as in 1 John or a different one. Many scholars interpret the reference to their 'going out into the world' as referring to missionary activity; they also see 2 Jn 9 as alluding indirectly to them: 'Anyone who goes ahead and does not remain in Christ's teaching does not possess God'.

Another likely polemical passage in 1 John is that which speaks of *testing the spirits*: 'By this you know the Spirit of God: every spirit which confesses Jesus Christ having come in the flesh is from God. And every spirit which does not confess Jesus is not from God' (4.2-3). This statement too is in the context of a warning against the Antichrist. It is reasonable to suppose that specific people are in mind. The author's designation of them as 'false prophets' (4.1) as well as 'antichrists' suggest they were Church leaders whose christological teaching he sees as erroneous. But it should be noted that he does not state their teaching and then refute it with arguments; rather he discredits his opponents by the use of pejorative language ('false prophets'; 'antichrists').

The affirmation (5.6) that Jesus came by both water and blood is also probably polemical. The author's strong insistence that Jesus did not come by water alone, but by blood must be aimed at someone, or some group, who denied this. We note the claim that it is the Spirit which bears witness, and the Spirit is truth. 1 John also contains a number of shorter christological affirmations, including the statements 'everyone who trusts that Jesus is the Christ is born from God' (5.1); 'whoever confesses that Jesus is the Son of God, God remains in that person, and that person in God' (4.15); and 'we have seen and bear witness that the Father has sent the Son, the Saviour of the world' (4.14). It is not so certain that these are polemical, since they could also be read as positive teaching, seeking to strengthen readers in the faith. The same applies to 1 John's final christological statement in 5.20 (to be discussed below, §5).

4. Attempts at Identifying the 'Opponents'

Apart from 'charismatics', four main groups of 'opponents' have been suggested. These overlap with one another in a quite complicated way, but we shall try to deal with them as concisely as possible.

Jews and Jewish Christians

Early this century A. Wurm proposed that 1 John's opponents were Jews who denied Jesus' messiahship, a hypothesis revived by O'Neill (1966). In support of this may be cited the references to those who deny that Jesus is the Christ (2.22), where the Greek could mean 'those who deny that the messiah is Jesus', and the positive affirmation that Jesus is the Son of God (4.15), where 'Son of God' could be a messianic title. But it is most unlikely that practising religious Jews would have been members, or former members, of a fully Christian community, as the 'opponents' must be. Nor can the 'opponents' be 'Judaizers', that is, Jewish Christians seeking to maintain their former practices, for there is no polemic against the Law, or circumcision, or other observances, such as one finds in other New Testament Epistles.

The author's polemic is christological. We should therefore be looking for a group who fail to adopt what the author would see as an 'orthodox' *interpretation* of Jesus' sonship and messiahship. We therefore turn to some groups criticized in the early Church as having 'unorthodox' Christologies.

Cerinthians

Cerinthus was a well-known Gnostic teacher (c. 100 CE), denounced by the second-century Church Fathers as a heretic. Eusebius cites from Irenaeus a story about Cerinthus and John. The two were in a bath-house at Ephesus. As soon as John knew that Cerinthus was there, he ran out for fear that the building might collapse as a divine punishment for Cerinthus's heresy (Irenaeus, *Adv. Haer.* 3.3.4). This apocryphal anecdote (a similar story is told about the gnostic Basilides and John) presupposes that John and Cerinthus are theologically opposed. Irenaeus and Jerome assume that the Gospel of John was written against Cerinthus, who is said to have believed that 'Christ' descended on a purely human Jesus at his baptism, making him divine, and departed from him at death. It is has been suggested that the confessions that Jesus has come *in the flesh* may be intended to affirm Jesus' true incarnation, as opposed to the idea that he only became Christ at his baptism. Supporters of this view include Westcott, Stott and, more tentatively, Bultmann. Against it may be argued the unreliability of patristic sources for Cerinthus's views; the fact that 1 John does not attack the idea that 'Christ' or the Spirit departed from Jesus at his death (if the insistence that Jesus 'came by blood' refers to this, then the allusion is quite opaque); and the absence of any references to Cerinthus's other reported teachings, for example, the idea that Jesus was the son of a Demiurge (an inferior creator-god). There is also no evidence that Cerinthus suffered from the ethical faults attributed to 1 John's opponents. For these reasons Schnackenburg, Marshall and others are probably right to reject the idea of Cerinthus as the principal adversary.

Docetists

Other scholars prefer to dub the opponents more loosely 'Docetists', without specific reference to Cerinthus (so, most recently, Schnelle). Docetism (from Greek *dokeō*, 'I seem') was a tendency in the early Church rather than a systematically argued doctrine (the name first appears in the writings of Serapion of Antioch, c. 190–203, but the tendency itself is probably earlier). Docetists considered the humanity and sufferings of Jesus to be apparent rather than real; some of them suggested Simon of Cyrene took Jesus' place on the cross. Important evidence comes from Ignatius of Antioch, who in his *Letter to the Smyrnaeans* gives thanks that his readers are firmly persuaded that Jesus was truly the Son of David *after the flesh*'; he was truly nailed (to the cross) *in the flesh*, truly suffered, and was 'in the flesh' after the resurrection (*Smyrn*. 1-3). In the same letter (*Smyrn*. 5.2) he speaks explicitly of him as 'flesh-bearer' (*sarkophoros*). In both this letter and that to the Trallians he denounces those who claim that Jesus only *appeared* (*dokeō*) to suffer (*Trall*. 9-10). Some of the christological passages we have cited (esp. 1 Jn 4.2; 5.6; and 2 Jn 7) *could* refer to such beliefs; for example, 5.6, with its affirmation that Jesus came by water and blood, might refer to his real baptism and death. But if our author is seeking to refute Docetism, he seems to be doing it very obscurely. One would have expected much more explicit references to Jesus' birth, death and resurrection, such as are found in Ignatius. There is also no evidence from 1 John that those attacked indulged in the 'judaizing' practices denounced by Ignatius as followed by the Docetists.

'Gnostics'

Gnosticism (from Greek *gnōsis*, 'knowledge') is a syncretistic way of thought, combining Jewish and Christian ideas with elements drawn from pagan philosophy (especially popular Platonism and Stoicism). A striking feature is its pervasive dualism in which the created world and material things generally are perceived as evil. Flesh is contrasted with spirit, and only some human beings are deemed to have the divine 'seed' or 'spark' which might bring redemption through knowledge. Among those who believe that the polemic of

1 John is directed against some form of Gnosticism are
Dodd, Kümmel, and Bogart. Dodd saw 1 John as reacting
against what he called the 'higher paganism' or 'Hellenistic
mysticism' of the Hermetic tracts (cf. above, Chapter 3 §5).
Kümmel thought some kind of Jewish Gnosticism was at
stake (1975: 225, 442), while Bogart argued 1 John was com-
bating a gnostic perfectionist sect (1977: esp. 115-22). The
main problem in tackling such theories is the varying ways
in which the authors use this elusive term 'Gnosticism'.
There are also difficulties over chronology, since the Nag
Hammadi codices (one of the main sources for Gnosticism)
postdate 1 John, being third to fifth centuries CE; even if we
postulate their original composition in the second century CE,
this is still later than any probable date for 1 John. The
Hermetic texts used by Dodd and the testimonies of the
Church Fathers on gnostic beliefs likewise postdate the
Johannines. All this means that rather than talking about
'Gnosticism' as such, it would be better to speak of 'incipient
Gnosticism' (or 'gnosis', as some scholars prefer).

The real difficulty with assuming that the author of 1 John
is reacting *against* incipient Gnosticism is that some of his
thought seems to be in harmony with it. His basic approach
is dualistic and he sees the *kosmos* as evil, telling his readers
not to love the world or the things of the world; he uses terms
like *sperma* and *chrisma*, which are known to have been
favoured by Gnostics, as if he were happy with them; he
stresses the importance of knowledge; he actually teaches
some kind of perfectionism. Those who wish to defend the
author's orthodoxy claim that he means something different
by these terms; they also argue that he believes firmly in the
incarnation. But he is treading a tightrope, and the suspicion
cannot be entirely allayed that he has gnostic leanings (cf.
Vouga: 380-81). He cannot be attacking fully-fledged
Gnosticism, for this does not yet exist; if he is attacking some
kind of incipient Gnosticism, he goes about it in a strange
way.

5. Some Alternative Views

The difficulties in identifying a single set of opponents have
led to the idea that more than one group may be involved.

Thus Smalley suggests that the Johannine community was split into three distinct groups: (a) Johannine Christians committed to the 'apostolic gospel'; (b) 'heretically inclined members from a Jewish background'; (c) 'heterodox followers from a Hellenistic (and/or pagan) background' (1984: xxiv). He sees 1 John as responding at times to one group, at times to another. The main problems with Smalley's view are lack of evidence for the heretically-inclined Jewish group; too sharp a differentiation between 'Palestinian and 'Hellenistic' Judaism; and too ready an attribution to this period of the categories 'orthodox' and 'heterodox'/'heretical'. Smalley is aware of the problems in using these labels, but this does not stop him employing them.

Brown sees 1 John's community as divided into just two groups: the epistolary author's adherents and his opponents (1982: 69). He believes 1 John was written, at a time of schism, to counter the opponents' misinterpretation of the Gospel. He argues that these opponents denied the importance of Jesus compared with the Spirit; that they refused to acknowledge that he was the 'Christ come in the flesh'; they failed to emphasize moral behaviour, claiming a perfectionist freedom from sin, and they did not love their fellow-Christians (1982: 47-68). Others who have argued that 1 John was written as a defence of the Gospel of John include Houlden (1973) and Wengst (1976). The strength of Brown's thesis is that it uses the text itself to determine the views of the 'opponents' rather than making them conform to groups known from outside sources. Its weakness lies in its over-ambitious reconstruction of their teaching, taking every possible statement as polemical, and the very hypothetical reconstruction of the history of the Johannine community. His theory also depends the chronological priority of the Gospel of John (which may be right; cf. Chapter 4, §4) and on the assumption that 1 John is polemical ethically as well as christologically (which this chapter challenges).

6. A Fresh Approach

All this suggests that perhaps the polemical character of 1 John has been exaggerated. Judith Lieu points out that there are no references to any 'schismatics' until 2.18, and that what 1 John says about them in no way proves that they are claiming superior 'spiritual' gifts (1981, 1991). She argues strongly that 1 John's primary concern is not to expose 'heresy' but to encourage readers and help them build up spiritual discernment. She believes it is methodologically unsound to conflate the moral antitheses with the christological confessions to provide the 'opponents' with a coherent ideology. While recognizing that there is polemic in 1 John, she does not believe it controls its thought. Pheme Perkins similarly advocates a 'less polemicized reading' of 1–3 John, arguing that critics have misread the situation when they see the Johannine community as violently torn apart. Our author's educational climate encouraged a rhetorical style which fostered antithetical and hostile language 'quite unlike anything we are used to. Personal attack, boasting, and challenges were all part of the on-going fabric of life' (1979: xxi-xxii). She believes that there is no evidence that the 'schismatics' had set up an opposition church. The most thorough-going non-polemical reading of 1 John is that of Dietmar Neufeld (1994). In a detailed analysis he argues that 1 John's purpose is to 'transform the readers' expectations, speech and conduct' (p. 133). 'The words of the text do not simply describe the author's or community's theological position, but enact belief' (p. 135).

What then are the beliefs about Jesus which our author is seeking to 'enact' or instil? First of all, he affirms Jesus as the Christ, the Son of God. But he means more than just that Jesus is the messiah. He is *uniquely* God's Son, in a way that other pious people are not (4.9). As Dunn (1989) has aptly recognized, the 'Son of God' confession in 1 John, as in the Gospel of John, is more 'highly rated' than in other New Testament texts. It implies a unique oneness with the Father. We note the repeated parallelism, effectively putting the Father and Son on a level of equality: 'Whoever confesses that Jesus is the Son of God, *God* remains in them and they in God' (4.15). 'Our fellowship is with the Father and with his Son Jesus Christ' (1.3). Those who deny Jesus Christ also deny the Father (2.22). God himself bears witness concerning his Son: 'And this is the witness, that God has given us eter-

nal life, and this life is in his Son. Whoever has the Son has
life; whoever does not have the Son does not have life' (5.11-
12). The Son gives life through his sacrificial death: his
'blood' is the means of the forgiveness of sins (1.7). This
atonement is not just for the Johannine community, but for
the sins of the whole world (2.2). Jesus' coming manifests
God's love (4.9) and destroys the works of the devil (3.8).
Those who trust that Jesus is God's Son conquer the world
(5.5).

An important christological affirmation comes at the end of
1 John: 'We know that the Son of God has come, and has
given us discernment, that we might know the True One;
and we are in the True One, in his Son Jesus Christ. This is
the true God and eternal life' (5.20). There has been much
debate about the referent for 'this' in the last sentence. Some
think it refers to God the Father (so Westcott, Brooke, Stott),
but this would be rather tautologous. Some believe it refers
to all that 1 John has been affirming (so Dodd), but
this would be an odd use of the masculine pronoun. Most
naturally 'this' is taken as referring to its immediate grammatical antecedent, namely Jesus Christ (so Bultmann,
Schnackenburg, Brown). If it is Jesus Christ who is described
as 'true God and eternal life', then we have an explicit affirmation of Jesus' divinity. Against this Grayston has argued
'it would be surprising if the writer...were now to ascribe full
deity to him in a throw-away line' (p. 147). But is this a
'throw-away line'? It reads more like a christological climax,
as suggested by the solemn opening 'we know', echoing two
previous assurances beginning with this same word.
Grayston believes that the end of 1 John reveals signs of
'improvisation and rhetorical haste'. But while it does not
equal the splendid perorations of classical oratory, the end is
hardly the 'ragbag' some have suggested. The author proclaims his purpose (v. 13): to let his audience know (*eidete*,
from the same verb as *oidamen*) that they have life in the
Son. He clarifies points which he feels he should have tack-
led; and reaffirms ideas previously enunciated, strengthen-
ing the confidence of his audience by the repeated *oidamen*,
'we know' (twice in v. 15, as well as in 18, 19 and 20). What
more fitting climax than to conclude by affirming directly

what he had hinted at in veiled manner, namely the divinity of Jesus (cf. Marshall)? It is frustrating that the ambiguity of the text makes this interpretation uncertain.

7. Conclusions

Attempts have been made to identify 1 John's 'opponents' as charismatics, Jews, Jewish Christians, Cerinthians, Docetists and Gnostics; but none of these identifications is fully convincing. This does not mean that 'opponents' did not exist, but only that the precise historical situation is not now recoverable. Methodologically, conflating all possibly polemical statements into a whole to reconstruct the adversaries' ideology is suspect, as the author may be aiming at more than one group; yet the more complicated the hypothesis, the less chance of its being right. The strongest case for polemics can be made for the christological 'confessions' and 'denials', together with the references to 'antichrists' and 'false prophets'. In his ethical teaching on love, obedience and the avoidance of sin, it is more likely the author of 1 John is directing his thoughts to his own community rather than outsiders or particular adversaries. It is true that 2 John includes warnings, apparently aimed at dissident missionary group, but 1 John is probably less polemical than often assumed (3 John contains no theological polemic). It therefore seems desirable to keep an open mind in approaching this text. The next chapter will seek to let 1 John speak in its own right, without any presuppositions about 'opponents', authorship or specific relationship to the Gospel of John.

Further Reading

In addition to the commentaries see:
J. Bogart, *Orthodox and Heretical Perfectionism in the Johannine Community* (Missoula, MT: Scholars Press, 1977).
P. Bonnard, *Les épitres johanniques* (Geneva: Labor et Fides, 1983).
Brown 1979
J.D.G. Dunn, *Christology in the Making* (London: SCM Press, 2nd edn, 1989), esp. pp. 56-60.
Kümmel 1979.
J. Lieu, 'Authority to Become Children of God', *NovT* 23 (1981), pp. 210-28.

—1991.

J.C. O'Neill, *The Puzzle of 1 John* (London: SPCK, 1966).

D. Neufeld, *Reconceiving Texts as Speech-Acts* (Leiden: Brill, 1994).

J. Painter, 'The "Opponents" in 1 John', *NTS* 32 (1986), pp. 48-71.

J.A.T. Robinson, 'The Destination and Purpose of the Johannine Epistles',
     NTS 7 (1960–61), 56-65 (arguing for a Jewish Christian background).

U. Schnelle, *Antidocetic Christology in the Gospel of John* (Minneapolis:
     Fortress Press, 1992).

F. Vouga, 'The Johannine School', *Bib* 69 (1988), pp. 371-85.

K. Wengst, *Häresie und Orthodoxie in Spiegel des ersten Johannesbriefes*
     (Gütersloh: Mohn, 1976).

R.A. Whitacre, *Johannine Polemic* (Chico: Scholars Press, 1982).

6

1 JOHN:
LEADING THEOLOGICAL IDEAS

IN THIS CHAPTER we study some of the leading theological
ideas of 1 John, paying attention to their context and their
potential rhetorical and pastoral purposes. The ideas will be
examined in the order in which they are presented by the
author, following the outline given earlier (Chapter 3 §2).

1. Prooemium or Opening Statement (1.1-4)

1 John begins with an elaborate Prooemium or Preface, quite
unlike the usual greeting at the start of a letter. Comprising
a single sentence, with 15 separate clauses, it is structurally
different from the simple paratactic style of the rest of the
Epistle, suggesting that it may have been added to the text
to give it weight and authority. The accumulation of five
clauses all beginning with the same word (*ho*, 'that which') is
designed to be impressive, while frequent use of verbs of perception—hearing, seeing, even touching—serves to reassure
and instil confidence. The Prooemium is couched in the first
person plural. Some have suggested that this is merely a
literary convention—an editorial 'we', or even a 'plural of
majesty'. More likely it is a genuine plural to denote a group
distinct from the readers, for example, eye-witnesses or tra-
dition-bearers who speak for the Johannine school. Grayston
writes: 'A Christian group addresses a group of readers in
formal language: they claim to possess an original disclosure
and experience and intend to communicate what they pos-

sess' (p. 33). The verbs 'we bear witness'...'we proclaim' have a performative character, and Neufeld rightly sees this Preface as a 'speech act'. The vivid language also reveals the depth of feeling.

But for all its impressiveness, the text is obscure. As Houlden remarks, 'Intensity of soul does not mean clarity of mind' (p. 46). What is meant by 'from the beginning' (*ap' archēs*)? Is it the beginning of creation (so Jn 8.44; cf. *en archē[i]*: Gen. 1.1; Jn 1.1), or of Jesus' ministry (cf. Jn 15.27; Lk. 1.2), or of the Church (cf. Acts 11.15)? Are the verbs relating to perception to be taken literally or metaphorically? And is the 'word of life' (*ho logos tēs zoēs*) to be understood as the pre-incarnate and incarnate Word (cf. Jn 1.1, 14), or the life-bringing message of, and about, Jesus (cf. Jn 6.68; Phil. 2.16)? Much depends on whether the Prooemium draws on the Gospel's Prologue. If it does, then a reference to Jesus as the eternal Logos might be possible; but it is hard to see why anyone should change the simple clarity of the Prologue into 1 John's rhetorical obscurity. If, however, we interpret the Prooemium from the rest of 1 John, the sense 'life-bringing message' for 'word of life' becomes more likely. For nowhere else in 1 John is *logos* personified; it is always used in the sense of preached (or spoken) word.

This encourages us to consider whether 'that which was from the beginning' might also refer to the preached word. Of the seven other examples of *ap' archēs* in 1 John, only one *must* signify the beginning of creation (3.8), though a further two might do so (2.13, 14). The remaining four (2.7; 24 *bis*; 3.11), together with the two examples in 2 John (vv. 5, 6), seem to refer to the beginning of the Gospel proclamation, though it is ambiguous whether the preaching of Jesus or that of the community is intended. The verbs of hearing readily apply to the Gospel message; those of seeing and touching less easily so—though a metaphorical sense is not impossible. The phrase 'the life was made manifest' (v. 3, with *phaneroomai*) might refer to the incarnation, but it could equally denote the revelation of eternal life in the preaching of Jesus. Possibly the passage is deliberately ambiguous (for a full discussion see Brown 1982: 154-70).

The Prooemium also introduces the important theme of

koinōnia, usually translated 'fellowship' or 'communion'. This word means 'participation' or 'sharing': it can be used of a business partnership (cf. Lk. 5.10); of sharing material goods (Rom. 15.26; 2 Cor. 8.4); or religious sharing, in faith, salvation, preaching, suffering, or sacrament (Phlm 6; Phil. 1.5; 3.10; 1 Cor. 10.16; Acts 2.42; cf. Rev. 1.9). J.P. Sampley (1980) has argued that it is also used in Paul as a technical term for a missionary partnership whereby a group offer material support to Paul in return for a share in the fruits of his endeavours, but *pace* Perkins (1983) that is not the meaning here. In 1 John's Prooemium the emphasis is on the 'community' which believers share with God the Father and Jesus Christ. The community which they share with one another is dependent on this, and upon their remaining in fellowship with God by being forgiven of their sins and 'walking in the light' (1.7). The concept of *koinōnia* or fellowship is striking, and contrasts sharply with the thought of the pagan philosopher Epictetus, who asks where could one ever find someone who thought they could have *koinōnia* with Zeus (*Discourses* 2.19.27). Although the language is different, the thought is not far distant from John's Gospel where Jesus speaks of himself as the Vine and his followers as the branches, urging them to remain in him and his love by keeping his commandments (Jn 15.1-10). In the Gospel, as in 1 John, union with Jesus means union also with God the Father (Jn 17.20-21).

The Prooemium ends with the hope that 'our' (or 'your') joy may be made complete (the MSS vary). Grayston sees these words as 'polite convention' (cf. 2 Jn 4; 3 Jn 4); but one suspects they are more than this. The concept of a faith that brings joy is common to John's Gospel (e.g. 15.11), the gnostic writings and Paul. Probably the mutual joy of author(s) and readers is intended; the warm associations of the words 'fellowship' and 'joy' serve to foster goodwill among the audience.

2. Main Body

Walking in the Light as a Sign of Fellowship with God (1.5–2.11)
(a) 1.5-10. The author declares his central theological premise: 'God is light and in him there is no darkness at all'

(v. 5). The same thought is enunciated both positively and negatively (a stylistic trait common to 1 John and the Gospel of John). While 'light' has many connotations in Jewish and Christian thought (e.g. glory, knowledge, revelation), it is evident from the context that God's holiness or goodness is intended. God is totally good, and the corollary is that those who would have fellowship with God must have nothing to do with 'darkness', that is, sin. But if they do sin, then they can receive forgiveness through Jesus Christ. These are key verses for showing the author's protreptic purpose—to warn his audience of the seriousness of sin.

(b) 2.1-6. A vivid vocative, 'little children', alerts readers to the importance of what follows. The author writes so that they may not sin; but if they do, he says, 'we have an Advocate with the Father, Jesus Christ the righteous'. This subsection develops a theme already flagged in 1.7, where the addressees were told that the blood of Jesus cleanses them from sin. Now in 2.1 they are further re-assured: Jesus is their advocate and an atoning sacrifice. Watson has argued that the author is employing the classical rhetorical technique of 'amplification', which serves both to invest its subject with dignity and to stress specific ideas by the use of strong, evocative words. He may be over-emphasizing the subtlety of our author's style, but the repetition certainly reinforces the message.

This subsection also contains the first of several tests for having fellowship with God (cf. above Chapter 3 §3). The author says: 'By this we know that we have known him, if we keep his commandments' (2.3). This introduces another recurrent theme—knowledge of God (cf. the emphatic statement in Jn 17.3, 'This is eternal life, that they should know you, the only true God...'). But what is meant by 'know'? Dodd argues that it denotes neither intellectual knowledge nor mystical experience (though it might include these); rather it harks back to concepts familiar from the Hebrew Bible (e.g. Jer. 9.3; 31.34), whereby knowledge of God involves being aware of God's saving actions for people, and of the need to respond with obedience (1946: 29-31). Thus it is not the same as the secret knowledge communicated to 'Gnostics': it implies ethical behaviour. That 1 John intends something like this is shown in v. 5: 'Whoever keeps his word, truly God's love is perfected in that person. By this we know that we are in him'. The ideas of 'knowing God' (2.3, 4), 'being in God' (2.5), and 'abiding in him' (2.6) are closely related; the term 'abiding' carries the connotation of perseverance (cf. Malatesta 1978). The purpose of 2.1-6 is then to encourage addressees and spur them to right conduct.

(c) 2.7-11. The address 'beloved' affirms community and affection between author and audience. It also heralds another of 1 John's great themes: the love of God. The author reminds addressees of the old commandment which they had 'from the beginning' (here unambiguously the beginning of the Gospel proclamation). He is so sure that they know what this commandment is that he does not need to quote it: he must be either citing common oral tradition or alluding to the Gospel of John (cf. 13.34; 15.12, 17). The term 'old' would have positive associations in a culture taught to value what was well established. But the author realizes the commandment is also new, because it was given in a new way by Jesus. So he partially corrects himself, adding a fresh idea: the commandment is also 'true' (*alēthēs*).

The concept of truth (*alētheia*) appeared already at 1.6, where it was said that those who claim fellowship with God while not 'walking in the light' lie and do not 'do the truth' (cf. 2.4). 'Doing the truth' corresponds to the Hebrew phrase *'asah 'emeth*, meaning 'to act loyally', and hence to act according to God's will: it occurs in the Hebrew Bible (e.g. Isa. 26.10), the Qumran texts (e.g. 1 QS 1.5), and in semitizing Greek (e.g. Gen. 32.11 LXX; Tob. 4.10; *T. Reub.* 6.9); it occurs only once elsewhere in the New Testament (Jn 3.21). 'Truth' in this sense has connotations of genuineness, reliability and integrity. The concept is prominent in John's Gospel, where truth is manifested through Jesus, and is even identified with him (Jn 1.17; 14.6 etc). In 1 John the two pairs of opposites—truth and falsehood, light and darkness—are frequently associated. Jesus' reliable new commandment is given because the darkness is passing away and the true light is appearing (cf. Jn 1.5). Cosmic and ethical dualism are thus combined. The section finishes with an antithesis: anyone who claims to be in the light but hates their 'brother', is still in the darkness (2.11). Specific individuals may be in mind, but more probably this is a general warning, aimed at inculcating consistency between what people claim and how they live. 'Doing the truth' means loving one's fellows.

Admonitions and Warning (2.12-17)
(a) 2.12-14. Six admonitions follow addressed respectively to 'children', 'fathers' and 'young men'. Brown has suggested that these might refer to different classes of Church members, with 'children' as the newly-baptized, 'fathers' as senior Church leaders, and 'young men' as junior Church officers; but evidence is lacking for such a technical understanding. From a modern viewpoint it is problematic that two of the three groups are addressed in exclusively masculine terms (attempts to show that 'fathers' and 'young men' are sexually inclusive have been unsuccessful). Watson's proposal (Chapter 3 §3) that the 'children' are the Johannine community as a whole, and the 'fathers' and 'young men' two constitutive classes, has much to commend it, though we need not go all the way with his elaborate analysis. But even if 'children' denotes all Church members, the references to 'fathers' and 'young men' (with no mention of 'mothers' and 'young women') is still androcentric. The address perpetuates the Jewish tradition that men constitute the religious assembly or at least its leadership. The Church today does not have to follow the same practice.

(b) 2.15-17. The admonitions serve as a transition to the next theme—not to love the world. 'The world' (*ho kosmos*), is a favourite Johannine term, occurring 24 times in 1–3 John, 78 times in John's Gospel, representing c. 57 per cent of the New Testament occurrences (in c. 15 per cent of the corpus). It is here used pejoratively (cf. Cassem 1972–73, stressing the tension between God's love of the world and denunciations against Christians loving it). Readers are also warned against the 'lust of the flesh' (with *sarx* used in a bad sense.) The dualistic contrast is strongly pointed between the world, which is passing away (like the darkness in 2.8), and those who do the will of God, who abide for ever.

3. *The 'Last Hour' and True Confession or Denial of Christ (2.18-27)*

The transitoriness of the world triggers the thought that it is now the 'last hour', and the expected Antichrist has come in the shape of those who departed from the community. They are called 'liars' and 'deceivers' because they deny that Jesus is the Christ. Perkins's claim that such strong language is typical of ancient oral literature should not blind us to the seriousness of the charge. 'Antichrist' here stands for the archetypal spiritual enemy of God. Though the name first occurs here, the concept is found in earlier Jewish and Christian literature (e.g. Dan. 11.36-7; 2 Thess. 2.3-8; Rev. 13; cf. Brooke: 69-79; Schnackenburg: 135-39; Jenks 1991). In our text a mythological concept has been historicized: human teachers with whom the author disagrees are identified with God's eschatological enemy. This is the language of polemic. These 'deceivers' are contrasted with the author's addressees, who are told they need no teacher, because they have an 'anointing from the Holy One' (probably here meaning God), giving them knowledge of everything (2.27).

The word *chrisma* here translated 'anointing' is puzzling. It derives from the verb *chriō*, meaning 'anoint', the same root as in 'Christ' and 'antichrist', giving a play on words. *Chrisma* appears only here in the New Testament. In secular Greek it is a concrete noun meaning 'ointment' or 'unguent'. In the LXX it is used in the phrase 'oil of anointing' in the consecration of priests, prophets and kings. The Church Fathers used it for the oil with which baptismal candidates were anointed, as well as for the act of anointing itself. Some have thought that in 1 John it denotes a sacramental act, possibly part of a baptismal rite (such as was practised by both Gnostics and orthodox Fathers). More probably *chrisma* is used metaphorically. We may compare the New Testament references to God's 'anointing' of Jesus with the Spirit (Lk. 4.18; Acts 4.27, 10.38). If that is the case, *chrisma* might be a distinctive image for the Spirit's work as teacher of truth (cf. the Paraclete in the Gospel of John). It may seem illogical for the author to say that his addressees need no teacher when he himself is teaching them, but probably he saw his own teaching as part of the 'anointing'. The idea that his pupils have

all knowledge may link up with the thought that they are living in the 'last days' when God had promised that he would
write his laws in his people's hearts and they would all know
him (Jer. 33.33-34; cf. also Isa. 54.13; Jn 6.45).

The Children of God and the Children of the Devil (2.28–3.24)
(a) 2.28-3.3. Mention of the 'last hour' reminds our author of
the parousia (Second Coming). Earnestly addressing his
readers as 'little children' (cf. 2.1), he urges them to abide
faithfully in Christ, so that they may have confidence when
he appears. They know that he is just, and everyone who acts
justly is born of him. This leads to the idea of the spiritual
birth of Christians. He exclaims in wonder at God's great
love that we should be called his children. Linking up with
the theme of the parousia, he says it has not yet been manifested what we shall be. But when he (God or Christ) is manifested, we shall be like him (3.2). The thought is awesome.
Therefore we must purify ourselves, as he is pure.
    (b) 3.4-10. Thus eschatology has been linked to ethics, and
the author returns to a well-worn theme—human sinfulness.
Jesus was 'manifested' to take away sins (3.5), being sinless
himself. Similar ideas were expressed earlier (1.7, 9; 2.1-2).
Curiously, the same Greek word *phaneroomai* ('be manifested') is used in 3.2-5 with three different meanings:
'appear' (of the parousia); 'be made clear' (of the future state
of Christians), and 'become visible' (of Christ's birth and ministry). The author now insists: nobody who abides in Jesus
sins. Earnestly he warns his readers: those who commit sin
are of the devil. Thus the familiar dualism is hammered
home, but the theme is amplified with a new thought: those
born of God *cannot* sin because God's *sperma*, 'seed', is in
them. The meaning of 'seed' is problematic: some refer it to
Jesus, as the 'seed' or offspring of God; some to the preached
Gospel ('sown' as the word); others see it as a designation of
the Holy Spirit (as in some gnostic texts). This last sugges-
tion seems most likely. The author provides no explanation,
but presses on with his antithesis: such people cannot sin
because they are born of God (see further Chapter 8). By this
the children of God and the children of the devil are manifested. Those who do not act righteously are not 'of God', nor

those who does not love their 'brother' (3.10). The last phrase reads like an afterthought, but it is the catchphrase which leads into the next subsection—on love.

(c) 3.11-18. A solemn opening introduces the passage: 'This is the message which you heard from the beginning, that we love one another', amplified by the new thought, 'not as Cain who murdered his brother'. The reference to Cain is often said to be the only specific Old Testament allusion in 1 John (so Marshall: 189); in fact, as Lieu (1993) has shown, Old Testament language and thought permeate our text. Cain's wickedness was a well-known theme in early Judaism (e.g. *T. Benj.* 7.5). In the gnostic *Valentinian Exposition* (11.38, NHL 440) Cain and Abel stand for all humanity, divided into evil and good. In 1 John, Cain's murderous hatred illustrates the hatred of 'the world' towards the Johannine community. Readers are warned not to marvel if the world hates them (cf. Jn 15.18). Is this a sign of a beleaguered and sectarian community (so Segovia)? Our author encourages his readers with the thought, 'We know that we have passed from death into life, because we love the "brothers"' (3.14). The language is that of 'realized eschatology' (cf. Jn 5.24): the true believers have already moved from the realm of death to that of life (cf. 1 Pet. 2.9; Rom. 6.1-11 etc.). Distinctive to 1 John is the idea that mutual love is proof of this passing from death to life. It leads the author on to the example of Jesus' sacrificial love: 'By this we know love, because he laid down his life for us' (3.16; cf. Jn 15.13). So readers are urged to love in action and truth. The teaching is illustrated by a telling example (3.17; cf. Jas 1.27; 2.14-17).

(d) 3.19-24. Returning to the theme of judgment the author speaks of confidence even if our heart condemns us. Is he thinking of people who know they have lapsed from his high ideal of love? He assures readers that God is greater than their hearts, and speaks of the power of prayer. But the logical sequence of thought is obscure. We are given a fresh definition of Christ's commandment: to believe in his Name and love one another. In our author's thought love and obedience are inextricably bound up together. But another new idea is quickly added: those who keep Christ's command abide in him, and he in them. By this we know that he abides in us, from the Spirit which he has given us (note the 'test formula').

The Two Kinds of Spirits (4.1-6)
Mention of the Spirit leads to the thought that not all who claim to speak from the Holy Spirit in fact do so. The author warns his beloved pupils not to trust every spirit but to test them, because 'many false prophets have gone out into the world' (4.1). The concept of false prophets is familiar from the Hebrew Bible and elsewhere in the New Testament; but this must allude to a contemporary situation in the Johannine community. Using the 'test formula' once again, the author says 'By this you know the Spirit of God: every spirit which confesses Jesus Christ come in the flesh is from God, and every spirit which does not confess Jesus is not from God'. This, he says, is the spirit of the antichrist. But he reminds his 'children' that they are of God and have conquered them (4.6). As a further test he adds: 'Those who know God listen to us, and those who are not of God do not listen to us. By this we know the Spirit of Truth and the Spirit of Deceit'. Once more those who are of God and those who are not are polarized (cf. Jn 8.43-7); the author is confident that he is on the right side. There is also a new idea—that of the two Spirits.

The Nature and the Demands of Love (4.7-21)
No catchword leads to the next section, though the affectionate 'beloved' may prepare readers for the injunction to love one another. There follows the profoundest and most moving part of this text where the nature of love is expounded (to be discussed in Chapter 7). This section culminates with the lapidary saying: 'We have this commandment from him, that those who love God love their brother also'.

Victory and Testimony (5.1-12)
Previously discussed themes are brought together and those of victory, divine begetting, and witness are developed. Everyone born of God is said to have conquered the world (cf. Jn 16.33; 1 Jn 2.13, 14). In an abrupt transition Jesus is said to be the one who came through water and blood, and 'the

Spirit, Water and Blood bear witness'. The theme of witness
has not appeared since the Prooemium. Some Latin manuscripts, and some Latin Church Fathers, read at this point
(5.8) a Trinitarian reference to the witness of the Father, the
Word and the Holy Spirit. This is the famous Johannine
'comma', which for centuries was used as a proof-text for
the Trinity. But the words are not found in the Greek manuscripts, and are demonstrably not original (hence their omission in virtually all modern texts and translations). They are
an early gloss which caught the imagination of the Latin
Church because of its doctrinal usefulness. The witness
does not just belong to God: it is also said to be within the
believer (v. 10; the Greek is obscure). The section ends with
a favourite Johannine theme, eternal life, and the stark
antithesis: 'Those who have the Son have eternal life; those
who do not have the Son of God do not have eternal life'
(5.12). The language is strongly reminiscent of John's Gospel
(cf. esp. 3.36).

3. Conclusion, Postscripts and Re-affirmation (5.13-21)

(a) 5.13. Some scholars believe that 1 John originally ended
here. 5.13 certainly reads like a conclusion on the purpose of
the Epistle: 'I have written these things to you that you may
know you have eternal life', with the loosely added explana-
tory phrase 'to those who believe in the Name of the Son of
God'. We are reminded of Jn 20.31. 'These things are written
so that you may believe that Jesus is the Christ, the Son of
God' with a similar tacked-on phrase 'so that believing you
may have life in his Name' (often thought to be the original
end of John's Gospel). But there is a subtle difference: the
Gospel is written so that people *may believe and have life*;
1 John so that believers may *know* they have eternal life.

(b) 5.14-17. Surprisingly, at this point, a new theme a
introduced: prayer. 'And this is the confidence (*parrhēsia*)
that we have before him, that if we pray according to his will,
he hears us' (5.14). This is not a doxology (as in Paul's
letters), but rather an exhortation (cf. the end of James). It
reads like a postscript. A further afterthought follows, dealing with a special case of intercessory prayer. In their final

sections both 1 John and James (5.19-20) mention prayer for a 'brother' who sins, but their teaching is different: James says that if a brother wanders (*planaomai*) from the truth, one should know that whoever turns a sinner from his wandering will save a life from death and 'cover' a multitude of sins. 1 John's message is more sombre: one should pray for such a person unless their sin is 'unto death' (5.16-17). If it is, the author does not encourage intercession (see further Chapter 8).

(c) 5.18-21. A brief conclusion follows: the author stresses that nobody born of God sins, and repeats his pessimistic belief that the whole world lies in the power of the Evil One; but he utters the encouraging thought that the Son of God has come and given us the ability to distinguish the True One. Attention has already been drawn to the ambiguity of the affirmation that follows: 'We are in the True One, in his Son Jesus Christ. This (or 'he') is the true God and eternal life.' (cf. Chapter 5 §6). The theme of eternal life makes an *inclusio* with the Prooemium. The final verse is a sharp warning: 'Little children, guard yourselves from idols'. While some scholars have taken this literally, most believe that 'idols' should be understood metaphorically of false teaching (cf. Chapter 3. §5 on Qumranic usage). Thus 1 John ends on the dualistic note with which the main text began: the contrast between the real God and falsehood.

4. Conclusions

We earlier quoted Houlden's words about 1 John insisting inflexibly upon a small number of points. This study rather suggests a rich mine of theological ideas, sometimes expressed in metaphorical and tantalizingly imprecise language. 1 John affirms God's nature as 'light', and the incompatibility of good and evil; it stresses the importance of a right Christology; it calls for love and obedience, and consistency between one's religious profession and practical conduct. Future judgment is expected, and the author believes that he is living in the end-time. The concepts of 'community', 'abiding', and 'being in' God/Christ all stress the close relationship of believers with the Father and the Son. The use of the terms *chrisma* and *sperma* suggests a vital role for the Spirit. The seriousness of sin, and Jesus' sacrificial and intercessory roles are major themes, as is the teaching on love. The Epistle combines encouragement, warning and polemic. In spite of its obscurities, one suspects it would have been effective in achieving its purposes.

Further Reading

In addition to the usual commentaries, see:

N.H. Cassem, 'A Grammatical and Contextual Inventory of the use of κόσμος in the Johannine Corpus with some implications for a Johannine cosmic theology', *NTS* 19 (1972–73), pp. 81-91.

H. Conzelmann, 'Was von Anfang war', in *Theologie als Schriftauslegung* (Munich: Chr. Kaiser Verlag, 1974), pp. 207-14.

C.C. Jenks, *The Origins and Early Development of the Antichrist Myth* (Berlin: de Gruyter, 1991).

J. Lieu, 'What was from the Beginning', *NTS* 39 (1993), pp. 458-77.

E. Malatesta, *Interiority and Covenant* (Rome: Biblical Institute, 1978) (on 'being in' and 'abiding in').

P. Perkins, '*Koinōnia* in 1 John 1.3-7', *CBQ* 45 (1983), pp. 631-41.

J.P. Sampley, *Pauline Partnership in Christ* (Philadelphia: Fortress Press, 1980).

F. Segovia, 'Love and Hatred of Jesus and Johannine Sectarianism', *CBQ* 43 (1981), pp. 259-72.

7

GOD'S LOVE AND
THE HUMAN RESPONSE

1. Divine Love and Human Love

THEIR TEACHING ON LOVE is one of the Johannines' most
attractive features. The theme is prominent in 1 John. First
appearing in 2.5, it recurs in 2.7-11, 15-17; 3.1-3, 10-18, 21-
23, and 5.1-3. The fullest treatment is 4.7-21, the so-called
'Hymn of Love' (so Klauck), seen by many as the heart of the
writing. The theme also appears briefly in 2–3 John.
Drawing on these materials one can construct a fairly coherent 'theology' of love; at the same time, we must be aware
that the texts are written for particular situations, and are
not intended as a systematic doctrinal exposition. There are
ambiguities in the phrase 'love of God' (e.g. 2.5), which can be
either an objective genitive, love for God, or subjective, God's
own love. Some passages are seriously obscure: for example,
5.1 might mean 'whoever loves the Father loves Christ' or
'whoever loves the Father loves their fellow-Christian', or
even, more generally, 'whoever loves the parent loves the
child'. These and other obscurities mean that our assessment
of the Epistles' theology must sometimes be provisional.

The author speaks of two kinds of love—God's for humanity, and human love for God; but these cannot be rigidly
separated. Probably the most famous text in the whole Bible
is 'God is love'—'the most comprehensive and sublime of all
biblical affirmations about God's being' (Stott), which occurs
twice in 1 John (4.8, 16), being unique to it. 1 John, like Paul
(Rom. 5.8), stresses that God loved us first (4.10, 19), and

showed this love in sending his Son to die, so that we might have life (4.9; cf. Jn 3.16). We know love through Jesus' laying down his life for us; in response we are called to lay down our lives for the 'brothers' (1 Jn 3.16). God's love is especially shown in the fact that believers are called his children (3.1; 4.7).

In the Johannines the proper response to God's love is love for others: sometimes this response is expressed by the use of 'we' with 'one another': 'Beloved, if God so loved us, we must love one another' (1 Jn 4.11-12; 2 Jn 5; cf. Jn 13.34; 15.12; 17), sometimes by the term 'brother' (*adelphos*): 'This is the commandment that we have from him, that those who love God should love their brother also' (4.21). The meaning of 'brother' has been much discussed. Does it denote 'fellow human being', with the idea of the community of all humanity? Or does it mean Christian 'brother'? And if the latter, is 'brother' used generically to include Christian women, or does the author have in mind Christian men? We shall return to these questions later.

The response to God's love involves obedience to his commands (1 Jn 5.2; cf. 2 Jn 6). Similar ideas are found in the Gospel's Supper Discourses (Jn 14.15, 21; 15.10-12). But what are God's commands? In 1 John it is clear that there is a double command to *faith* and *mutual love*: 'This is his command that we believe in the Name of his Son Jesus Christ and that we love one another' (3.23; this is probably true of the Gospel also: von Wahlde 1990). Faith is not so much intellectual assent (which one cannot produce at will) as trust, commitment and 'a receptive attitude' (so Schlatter). The second command, to love, is, as Schnackenburg says, secondary to the first and a necessary consequence of it. Such love, 1 John insists, must be real, and not just verbal: 'Little children, let us not love in word or tongue, but in deed and truth' (3.18). The phrase 'in truth' does not mean just 'in fact'; it rather suggests love in accord with reality (so Marshall: 196; cf. Chapter 6 §2.1.c on 'truth'). The very practical nature of this 'brotherly' love is illustrated by a moving example: 'If anyone has the necessities of life and sees their "brother" in need and shuts up their compassion from him, how does God's love abide in that person?'

(3.17). This last saying also shows that the human response to God's love must involve love for others. One may compare 4.21: 'We have this command from him, that those who love God should love their "brother" also'.

Love for God excludes love for 'the world' and 'the things in the world'. These are described as 'the desire of the flesh, the desire of the eyes, and the boastfulness of life' (2.16). The use of such emotive terms as *epithymia* and *alazoneia* suggests that the author has in mind sensual cravings, ruthless greed, and the pretentiousness of material success, rather than the physical world in general. But he may also be thinking of the transitoriness of created things (2.17). The thought is close to Jas 4.4. 'Friendship with the world is enmity towards God'.

1 John also speaks, in striking language, of the *results* of mutual love: 'We know that we have crossed out of death into life, because we love the "brothers"' (3.14); conversely anyone who hates a 'brother' is a 'murderer' (*anthrōpoktonos*, a strong and rare word used for special emphasis); such people have no life in them (3.15). But those who stand firm in their love, have God's abiding presence. They have confidence in judgment, because 'perfect love casts out fear' (4.18).

2. The Language of Love

Before proceeding further it is worth considering in more detail what is meant by the word 'love'. For modern readers it suggests an emotion. We use it for strong affection for parents, children, brothers and sisters; for the powerful and abiding love of wife and husband; for the mutual attraction of a man and a woman; for some people it may include intensely felt same-sex relationships. In English, the word 'love' can convey any of these ideas, and often the meaning has to be indicated by an epithet, such as 'sexual', 'marital', or 'parental'. Greek has a wide range of words to express the concept of love: *erōs*, used mostly for sexual love; *philia*, usually affection and friendship; *storgē*, a more neutral word for natural affection; *pothos* and *himeros*, meaning yearning and longing; and *agapē*, used by New Testament writers pre-eminently for Christian love, including both God's love for humanity and human love for God. In 1–3 John the idea of 'love' is expressed exclusively by *agapē* (21×) and its cognate verb *agapaō* (31×) and adjective *agapētos*, 'beloved' (10×). In 1 John two-thirds of the occurrences of these words occur in the section 4.7-5.3 (John's Gospel uses both *agapaō* and *phileō*, apparently as synonyms).

Much has been written on the word *agapē*. Nygren (1932–39) and Spicq (1958–59) each devoted a three-volume work to it. It has sometimes been claimed that the noun is a Christian creation, or at the very least part of the specialized vocabulary of early Christian literature—'the last stronghold of the old conception of a special biblical Greek' (Tarelli). Thus Thayer's 1890 *Lexicon* describes *agapē* as 'a purely biblical and ecclesiastical word' (so too Souter in his *Pocket-Lexicon*, 1920). Often a sharp distinction is drawn between Christian *agapē* and pagan *erōs* (cf. Nygren 1932: 23-27). Serious objections may be made to these ideas. First, *agapē* is not an exclusively Christian word: it appears, with its cognate *agapēsis*, not infrequently in the LXX and other Jewish writings (e.g. *Aristeas*, Philo, *Testaments of the Twelve Patriarchs*). It is true that Deissmann's reading of *Agapē* as a title of Isis (*P. Oxy* 1380) has been disputed; but in two important studies Ceresa-Gastaldo has shown that there are at least four other certain, and several further possible, examples of *agapē* in secular papyri uninfluenced by the Bible. It is used for love of one's country; kindness or favour; marital love; and as a female proper name.

Secondly, the use of the abstract noun *agapē* cannot be separated from that of the cognate verb *agapaō*. This occurs already in the earliest Greek literature (Homer) with the meaning 'welcome with affection' (cf. *agapazō*). *Agapaō* is used throughout the classical age covering a wide semantic field, including 'to love one's children', 'to show affection for the dead', and 'to be pleased, contented, or fond of'. Beginning in the fourth century BCE, as Joly has ably shown, *agapaō* gradually replaced *phileō* as a general verb expressing affection. One factor may have been a shift of meaning in *phileō*, which takes on the sense of 'kiss', as in Modern Greek. Schnackenburg's assertion (p. 213) that *agapaō* 'was hardly ever used for human love in Greek' is inaccurate. (Joly 1968 cites multiple examples from Demosthenes, Isocrates,

Aristotle, Polybius, Plutarch *et al.*)

Thirdly, as Barr has stressed, one must be wary of assuming that words always carry the same connotations. It is just not true that *agapē* always denotes affectionate love with no sexual overtones. In the LXX it is used for Amnon's incestuous lust for Tamar (2 Kgdms [= 2 Sam.] 13.15); for erotic heterosexual love in the Song of Songs (e.g. 2.4-5; 5.8); for David's love for Jonathan; and metaphorically for Yahweh's love for Israel as his 'wife' (Jer. 2.2). The cognate noun *agapēsis* is used both for prostitution (Jer. 2.23) and for God's eternal love (Jer. 38.3 LXX = 31.3 MT; cf. Hos. 11.4). Ceresa-Gastaldo has suggested that the bridge between this wide-ranging LXX usage and the narrower New Testament use is Hellenistic-Jewish literature. The *Letter of Aristeas*, which uses a purported dialogue between the Egyptian king and the translators of the LXX as a means of moral instruction, speaks of love (*agapē*) as a gift from God (cf. 1 Jn 4.7). The Book of Wisdom (6.17-18) states: 'The beginning of wisdom is the truest desire for instruction; concern for instruction is love (*agapē*) [of wisdom]; love is the keeping of her laws; attention to [her] laws is assurance of immortality; immortality brings one near to God'. This is an example of an ancient rhetorical figure known as a sorites, in which different concepts are equated with one another in a chain until a climax is reached. Though much longer and more loosely structured, 1 John's 'Hymn' (4.7-21) contains a similar series of interrelated statements beginning and ending with the theme of mutual love. 1 John and Wisdom share common themes in their linking of love and obedience, and the idea that obedient love brings one near to God.

In commenting on *Aristeas*, Meecham argued that Alexandrian Hellenistic writers 'purged' *agapē* from its 'carnal associations' and thus paved the way for New Testament usage (1965: 63). One should, however, be wary of the word 'purge': *agapaō* continued to be used in an erotic sense in secular literature. Curiously, *erōs* and its cognates followed a similar development; from connoting passionate sexual love, they came to be used of the love of wisdom (e.g. Plato, *Phaedo* 66e; Wis. 8.2) and, in the Church Fathers, of Christian mutual love—and even of God's love. The evidence thus suggests that *agapaō* and cognates were accessible to New Testament authors as part of the regular vocabulary of Hellenistic Greek, both secular and religious-philosophical.

3. God is Love

The heart of 1 John's teaching is that 'precious gem' (Loader), 'God is love' (1 Jn 4.8, 16). This has been the theme of so much exposition and preaching that it is hard to discuss. It has been seen as making a definitive statement about God's nature and as a 'high peak' of divine revelation in Scripture. Dodd writes: 'To say "God is love" implies that *all* His activity is loving activity. If He creates, He creates in love; if He rules, He rules in love; if He judges, He judges in love. All that He does is an expression of His nature, which is—to love' (1946: 110).

Dodd's words are profoundly moving; but can we deduce all this from the text? The statement 'God is love' parallels two other Johannine sayings—'God is light' (1 Jn 1.5), and 'God is spirit' (Jn 4.24). Marshall (p. 212) has pointed out that there is nothing in the nature of the love saying to suggest that it is 'superior' to other New Testament sayings about God's nature. It is paralleled by the stern statement in Heb. 12.29 (cf. Deut. 4.24: 'our God is a consuming fire'), which the author uses to induce reverent awe and to warn against apostasy. 1 John's statements about God's nature also have affinities with the 'I am' sayings of John's Gospel and Revelation, where similarly we have a subject (the pronoun 'I'), the verb to be, and an abstract noun as complement, for example, 'I am the resurrection and the life' (Jn 11.25). The noun may also be a concrete one (e.g. bread, vine) used metaphorically. We can no more deduce from the statement 'God is love' that every single activity of God is done in love than we can deduce from 'I am the bread of life' that every activity of Jesus is concerned with feeding.

We have to recognize that the Johannine authors were fond of vivid metaphorical and abstract formulations, such as are indeed found in pagan and gnostic literature, e.g. the Hermetic, 'I am that light, *Nous*, your God' (cited above, Chapter 3 §5). But our author is not engaging in

philosophical speculation or Hellenistic mysticism. The
Johannine statements are different from the abstruse specu-
lations of developed Gnosticism. 'God is love' in 1 Jn 4.8 is
immediately followed by a reference to God's action: 'In this
the love of God was manifested among us, that God sent his
only Son into the world, so that we might live through him'
(4.9). Similarly, 'God is love' in 4.16 leads into an affirmation
of God's abiding presence with those who love.

The Johannine predications about God are inseparable
from their implications for human behaviour. Thus 'God is
light' (1.5) entails the need for God's people to behave in
accordance with God's nature; 'God is spirit' (Jn 4.24) leads
into the need to worship 'in spirit and in truth'. The assurance 'God is love' brings with it the imperative that those
who would be God's children must love one another. Thus,
while Dodd may be going beyond 1 John's thought in assert-
ing that *all* God's activity is carried out in love, he is right
that Divine love manifests itself in action.

In this belief our author is true to his Jewish roots. It is
popularly assumed that the idea of God as love is a special
'New Testament' insight, whereas the 'Old Testament' teaches of God's wrath. This is not the case. The writers of the
Hebrew Bible regularly speak of God's love, sometimes using
abstract nouns (e.g. $\jmath ab^a bah$; $hesed$; $rah^a mim$), sometimes by
describing his beneficent actions (e.g. in rescuing Israel from
Egypt). People sometimes fail to appreciate how often the
Hebrew Bible refers to God's love because they search
English concordances under the word 'love', without realizing
that God's loving nature is also depicted by such terms as
'mercy', kindness', 'goodness' (cf. Snaith 1944: 94-142). In the
Hebrew Bible God's love is especially shown in the Covenant,
which requires a response from God's people: 'Know that the
Lord your God is God, the faithful God who keeps covenant
and steadfast love with those who love him and keep his
commandments...' (Deut. 7.9). Though the term 'covenant' is
absent from 1 John, the idea of mutual obligation is not. As
Malatesta has strongly argued, the concept of a new
covenant in people's hearts underlies much of 1 John's
speech about God's in-dwelling presence in those who love
him, and their response of obedience.

4. Mutual Love as a Response to God's Love

The demand for a response to God's love is expressed in many different ways in 1 John (see 2.15-17; 3.11-18, 23; 4.7-21; 5.1-3). An important text shaping its thought is the Deuteronomic *shema* (Deut. 6.4-5): 'Hear, O Israel: the LORD our God is one LORD; and you shall love the Lord your God with all your heart, and with all your soul, and with all your might' (Deut. 6.4-5). Here the affirmation 'God is one' defines how God may be known and calls for a response (cf. Grayston). The Levitical command to love one's neighbour is likewise rooted in God's character: 'You shall love your neighbour as yourself: I am the LORD' (Lev. 19.18; cited some eight times in the Hebrew Bible). It is often thought that 'neighbour' in this text denotes only 'fellow Jew', but one should read on to v. 34. 'The alien who resides with you shall be to you as a citizen among you; you shall love the alien as yourself; for you were aliens in Egypt. I am the Lord your God'. We note again the grounding of the command in God's nature and saving activity.

An even more important antecedent to 1 John's teaching on love is Jesus' summary of the Law in the double 'love command' (Mk 12.28-34; Mt. 22.34-40; Lk. 10.25-28). Jesus is not unique here—there are parallels in the *Testaments of the Twelve Patriarchs* (e.g. *T. Iss.* 5.2; 7.6), but it is virtually certain that 1 John's teaching derives from the Gospel tradition. However, it may not stem directly from Jesus himself. It is more probable that our author draws on Jesus' teaching as mediated through the Johannine 'school'. We observe the reformulation of the second part of the 'love command' from love of *neighbour* to love of *one another* (cf. Jn 13.35 etc) or to love of *the brothers* (see further Furnish; Perkins). Yet the language with which 1 John speaks of love is closely similar to that of the Gospel of John: note especially the unusual phrase (*psychēn tithenai*, 'lay down' (lit. 'place') one's life (3.16; cf. Jn 15.13). Either our author was familiar with the teaching on love in the Supper Discourses (so Brown), or he had access to a tradition very close to them.

5. Problems with 'Brotherly' Love

From the time of Augustine 1 John's teaching on love has been regarded as the Epistle's supreme contribution to Christian theology. It has rightly been compared to Paul's great 'hymn' (1 Cor. 13), and has been used as a foundation by those seeking to write a biblical theology of love (cf. Nygren; Spicq; Outka). But it is not without its problems. Many people have seen in it a *restriction* of Jesus' love command. In the Synoptic tradition Jesus teaches that 'neighbour' is not confined to fellow Jew, but includes even a hated Samaritan (Lk. 10.29-37). The Sermon on the Mount specifically enjoins love of enemies (Mt. 5.43-48; cf. Lk. 6.27-31). Jesus' whole life exemplifies love of the loveless. But nowhere in the Johannine literature is there a reference to love for enemies, or even strangers. The 'brothers' so frequently mentioned appear to be members of the Johannine community who are in accord with the author's own teaching. The most extreme critic is J.T. Sanders, who sees Johannine ethics as weak and morally bankrupt. A Johannine Christian, he says, on seeing a wounded traveller would ask 'Are you saved, brother?', instead of giving aid (*Ethics of the New Testament* [2nd edn, 1986]: 100).

Too much should not be made of the change from the Synoptic 'neighbour' to Johannine 'brother' or 'one another': these terms are often used as synonyms in Jewish and Christian Greek (e.g. Gal. 5.13-15). It is possible, as Robinson and others have argued, that in the Johannine 'brother' and 'one another' may include fellow human beings. But even if we follow the majority of scholars who think they mean primarily 'fellow Christians', we still must reply to Sanders that the Johannines nowhere suggest that a Johannine Christian would neglect a dying stranger. Such a basic duty of Jewish and Christian piety would have been taken for granted. 1–3 John are not concerned with enunciating a complete Gospel, but rather dealing with particular situations. Their community is divided and failing in certain basic areas of faith and practice; the texts focus on the most urgent need—mutual love among the committed.

What of attitudes to dissentients? In the modern climate of

ecumenism and inter-faith dialogue the Johannine Epistles may seem intolerant and uncharitable. In interpreting them, we have to understand the importance for their author(s) of a right understanding of Jesus' person, and the indissoluble connection between right belief and right conduct. The secessionists (if such they be) were seen as the equivalent of idolaters. To offer them friendship was to affirm their false beliefs. To share a meal with them was to participate in their sin (2 Jn 11; cf. 1 Cor. 10.20; 2 Cor. 6.14). This may help explain the strange teaching at the end of 1 John that it is not worth praying for somebody who has sinned 'unto death'. We shall reserve till our last Chapter how such ideas might be interpreted today.

6. Sexism in the Johannine Epistles?

Throughout this discussion we have referred to 'brother' and 'the brothers'—a literal rendering of Greek words used. But does 'brothers' include 'sisters'? The Greek noun *adelphos* is used for a blood-brother, for a fellow-member of a community, or occasionally for a fellow human being (e.g. Gen. 9.5). In the plural it can be inclusive, denoting siblings (cf. German 'Geschwister'). The NRSV renders it throughout as 'brothers and sisters', but this unduly stresses the supposed presence of women. There is no way of telling whether or not the author(s) had them in mind when writing. Masculine terminology predominates in the admonitions of 1 Jn 2.12-14 (though 'children' could be inclusive). Ancient philosophical schools sometimes included women, but not always. There were women among Jesus' disciples, but the Twelve were all men and some of his teaching appears to be given exclusively to them. Some Pauline letters and 1 Peter contain injunctions directly addressed to women, but Galatians with all its references to circumcision seems to be primarily aimed at men (I owe this point to Judith Lieu). If the Johannine authors had wanted to include women specifically they could have done so: compare James's reference to a 'brother or a sister' (*adelphos ē adelphē*) in need (Jas 2.15) and Jesus' saying in Mark (3.35) that whoever does the will of God is his 'brother and sister and mother'. In contrast, 1–3 John nowhere explicitly mention women (unless 2 John's 'elect lady' and her 'sister' are real women). We must therefore conclude that, by modern standards, the formulation of 1–3 John's teaching is androcentric in that males are perceived as the norm, though it is probably too much to call it 'sexist'. One hopes that the author(s), if pressed, would agree that all that is said about love, faith, and obedience applies also to Christian women.

7. Conclusion

Their teaching on love is indeed one of the most important contributions that the Johannines can make to Christian theology and ethics. Their insight that Christian love is grounded in Divine love is fundamental. The recognition that love is inconsistent with fear is a valuable testimony in the face of many religions which build precisely on fear. Their insistence that those who claim to love God must also show love to their fellows is a clarion call against hypocrisy; and even if 'brother' is understood in a narrow sense, this does not preclude a wider application (cf. 1 Thess. 3.12; 5.15; Gal. 6.10).

Further Reading

J. Barr, *The Semantics of Biblical Language* (London: SCM Press; Philadelphia: Trinity Press International, 1961), ch. 8.

A. Ceresa-Gastaldo, '*Agapē* in Documents Earlier than the NT', *Aegyptus* 31 (1951–52), pp. 269-306.

—'*Agapē* in Documents outside Biblical Influence', *Rivista di Filologia Classica* 31 (1953), pp. 347-56 [both in Italian].

V.P. Furnish, *The Love Command in the New Testament* (Nashville: Abingdon Press, 1972).

W. Harrelson, 'The Idea of Agape in the NT', *Journal of Religion* 31 (1951), pp. 169-82 (criticizing Nygren).

R. Joly, *Le vocabulaire chrétien de l'amour est-il original?* (Brussels: Presses Universitaires, 1968) (criticizing Spicq).

E. Malatesta, *Interiority and Covenant* (Rome: Biblical Institute, 1978).

H.G. Meecham, *The Letter of Aristeas* (Manchester: Manchester University Press, 1935).

J. Moffatt, *Love in the New Testament* (London: Hodder, 1929).

A. Nygren, *Agape and Eros* (3 vols.; London: SPCK, 1932–39), esp. I.

G. Outka, *Agape* (Yale: Yale University Press, 1972).

P. Perkins, *Love Commands in the New Testament* (New York: Paulist Press, 1982).

J.A.T. Robinson, *The Priority of John* (London: SCM Press, 1985), esp. 329-33.

A. Schlatter, *Der Glaube* (Stuttgart: Calwer Verlag, 6th edn, 1982), esp. p. 218.

M. Silva, *Biblical Words and their Meaning* (Grand Rapids: Zondervan, 1983), esp. p. 96.

N.H. Snaith, *Distinctive Ideas of the Old Testament* (London: Epworth, 1944), esp. pp. 94-130.

C. Spicq, *Agapè dans le Nouveau Testament* (3 vols.; Paris: Gabalda, 1958–59), esp. III on 1–3 John.

—*Notes de lexicographie néotestamentaire*, I (Göttingen: Vandenhoeck & Ruprecht, 1987), pp. 16-30.

C.C. Tarelli, '*Agapē*', *JTS* 51 (1950), pp. 64-67.

J.H. Thayer, *Grimm's Greek–English Lexicon of the New Testament* (Edinburgh: T. & T. Clark, rev. edn, 1980).

U. von Wahlde, *The Johannine Commandments* (New York: Paulist Press, 1990).

8

SIN, FORGIVENESS,
JUDGMENT AND ESCHATOLOGY

1. Introduction

IF WE HAD ONLY the first two chapters of 1 John, its teaching on sin might seem fairly straightforward. God is 'light', i.e. perfect goodness (cf. Chapter 6 §2.1); those who are God's children must 'walk in the light', that is, behave in conformity with God's demands. If they fail, they must confess their sins and God will forgive them. This forgiveness is effected through the death of Jesus (1.7-9). He is their champion (*paraklētos*) with the Father and atones for the sins of the whole world (2.1-2). However, even these apparently simple statements raise questions. How can Jesus' death enable God to forgive sins? Was there no means of forgiveness before his self-sacrifice? Did he die as our representative or our substitute? And how can he expiate the sins of the whole world, if the whole world does not repent? To understand 1 John's thought we need to investigate the Jewish background.

2. Sacrifice and Forgiveness

Ancient Judaism had an elaborate system of sacrifices which could be offered in thanksgiving or fulfilment of vows, as an earnest of repentance and reparation for sin, as a sign of self-dedication or as a means of reconciliation with God (see Carpenter 1988). Such sacrifices often involved shedding animal blood (a symbol of their life). There was also the special rite of the Day of Atonement when the High Priest entered the Holy of Holies and made sacrifice for his own sins and the unwitting sins of the people by sprinkling blood on the *hilastērion* ('mercy-seat'). Very early, the Christian Church saw the death of Jesus an atonement, replacing this complex system of Jewish rituals (cf. Mk 10.45; Rom. 3.25; 1 Cor. 11.25; 1 Pet. 1.18-19); the theology is worked out in most detail in Hebrews 7–10.

The author of 1 John works within this frame of understanding. Jesus' *blood* cleanses from sin (1.7); he was manifested (*phaneroomai*) to 'take away' sins (3.5); and is an atoning sacrifice (*hilasmos*) (2.2; 4.10). There has been a long and arid controversy over whether *hilasmos* (together with the related term *hilastērion* in Rom. 3.24) means 'propitiation' (rendering God favourable) or 'expiation' (wiping out sins and their effects) (see the standard dictionaries and commentaries). The main point is that 1 John, in common with most of the rest of the New Testament authors, perceives the need for an objective sacrifice to be made in order for God to forgive sins—in this case the death of Jesus.

But Jesus is not only the sacrificial victim; he is also the one who intercedes with the Father. In 2.1 he is called an 'advocate' or 'champion' (*paraklētos*), a term found only in John's Gospel and 1 John among New Testament writings (see further Grayston 1981). One might wonder why such intercession is necessary if Jesus' death constitutes a 'full, perfect and sufficient sacrifice' (Book of Common Prayer); but the idea seems to be that since human beings regularly sin— even those who have been converted, put their trust in Christ, and become God's children—a heavenly intercessor is needed to continue to plead for them. In John's Gospel the 'paraclete' is the Holy Spirit (Spirit of Truth) who serves as Jesus' successor after his departure from earth, guiding his disciples (14.16-17; 15.26; 16.7-15); in 1 John 'paraclete' refers to Jesus himself. The Gospel's image of the Spirit as 'advocate' is close to that of Paul in Rom. 8.26, when he speaks of the Spirit interceding 'with sighs too deep for words', while 1 John's is closer to that of Hebrews (e.g. 7.25; cf. Rom. 8.34), where Jesus is intercessor. The tension between the two Johannine writings may not be so great as sometimes supposed, because the idea of Jesus as 'paraclete' may be implied in the Gospel reference to the Spirit as *'another* paraclete' (14.16); and John's Gospel does, in fact, depict Jesus as intercessor, notably in the 'high priestly' prayer of ch. 17. On the other hand, 1 John displays no knowledge of the Gospel's developed doctrine of the Spirit as a personal being. It is a matter of radical concern how this teaching about sacrifice and intercession may be understood and applied in the modern world.

3. Future Judgment

In early Christian thought Jesus is not only the sacrifice for sin; he is also the one appointed by God as future judge (Jn 5.28-29; Acts 10.42 etc.); the Synoptic Gospels and other New Testament writings see this as taking place at his *parousia* (lit. 'presence' or 'arrival') in power and glory to gather his Elect (Mk 13.26-7; Mt. 24.30-1; 2 Thess. 2.1-12 etc.). Do the Johannines also have this expectation? The evidence is not completely clear. 2 Jn 7 speaks of deceivers who do not 'acknowledge Jesus Christ coming in the flesh'. If the present participle *erchomenon,* 'coming', is given its normal grammatical force this must either refer to the present time (which makes no sense) or be used futuristically (a common usage). In that case the author is referring to a future coming of Jesus (presumably as judge). Such a view is taken, among others, by Vouga. But since there is no other evidence that a 'fleshly' second coming was controversial, most commentators assume that the author intended to say 'having come', with reference to the incarnation (cf. 1 Jn 4.2; Polycarp, *Phil.* 7.1—both using past tenses). If that is his meaning, 'our author is not skilled in the niceties of Greek idiom' (Dodd 1946: 149).

A future coming is more frequently seen in 1 Jn 2.28–3.3, referring to 'his' *parousia* and future manifestation. Unfortunately all the key phrases are ambiguous: the author has just spoken of the *chrisma* which teaches his protégés, and bids them 'abide in it/him', so that if (or 'when') it/he is manifested they may have confidence and not be ashamed. The vocabulary is that of judgment; the problem is that the subject of 'be manifested' (*phaneroomai*) is obscure. It could be either neuter or masculine. Grammatically it ought to refer to the *chrisma* (neuter); but even if the 'anointing' has rightly been identified with the Holy Spirit, it is difficult to believe that the author intended an eschatological manifestation of the Spirit in this way. From what follows, the subject of *phaneroomai* must be God or Christ—but which?

Further ambiguities arise in the next verses: according to the commonly accepted text, the author says, 'Beloved, we are now children of God, and it has not yet been manifested (*phaneroomai*) what we shall be. We know that if (or 'when') he is manifested, we shall be like him, because we shall see him as he is' (3.2). It is uncertain in both 2.28 and 3.2 whether *ean* has its usual meaning of 'if' (implying a contingency), or whether it should be rendered 'when' (implying certainty). Grammatically 'he' in v. 3 ought to refer to God (the last noun named), but since our author is not distinguished for his good Greek, many commentators think he must be referring to *Jesus'* 'second coming' (cf. Mt. 24.3; 1 Cor. 15.23).

Against this Grayston has argued, on theological grounds, that *God* is intended. He sees Christ's 'disclosure' (a term he prefers to 'manifestation') as occurring through his incarnation and preaching, which effectively judges people as they accept or reject him. Believers have already passed from death to life (1 Jn 3.14). There is no need for any further *parousia* of Jesus. Final judgment, in his view, belongs to God, whose future parousia in judgment is well attested in the Hebrew Bible and Judaism (Grayston 1984: 95-97; cf. O'Neill 1966: 32-36). The view has merits in that it saves Jesus being victim, intercessor and judge; it relieves the tension of the 'realized' and 'final' eschatology; it also avoids the awkwardness of 2.29, which speaks of those who act righteously being born 'from him', where the only antecedent is the one who may appear. If this is Jesus, we have an idea not otherwise attested in the New Testament that believers are born from Jesus; whereas if God is the source of the birth, this harmonizes with a widespread New Testament concept (cf. 1 Pet. 1.3; Jas 1.18), occurring frequently in 1 John (cf. also Jn 1.13). However, it must be admitted that the whole section is fraught with difficulty, and small changes to an insecure punctuation could alter the meaning radically (see Synge 1952).

These matters have been treated at length to illustrate the difficulties in discovering 1 John's precise meaning. Similar problems occur with many other passages: in 3.19-20, for example, it is not clear whether the author is assuring readers that God is less accusing than their hearts, or warning them that God is more severe. However, the main burden of 1 John's thought seems to be this: there will be future judgment (whether by God or Jesus); believers should have confidence in the face of this; God (or Jesus) is reliable and just, and will forgive them their sins, as long as they confess them. Meanwhile they should love one another, keep God's (or Jesus') commandments, and purify themselves as 'he' is pure: when they see 'him' they will be transformed to be like 'him'. This last idea has often been thought to derive from Hellenistic mysticism, but is found also in Judaism.

4. Sin and Sinlessness

In the first half of 1 John (1.5–3.3) the author's basic meaning was fairly clear, though some details remained obscure. In the second part (3.4–5.12) things get more complicated. The main purpose seems to be to stress the seriousness of sin. 'Whoever commits sin (*hamartia*) also commits lawlessness' (3.4). 'Lawlessness' (*anomia*) may be regarded as more heinous than 'sin', being a sign of the spiritual rebelliousness characteristic of the end-time (cf. 2 Thess. 2.3-7; Mt. 24.11-12). In Jewish thought a sharp contrast is often drawn between 'lawless' and ungodly sinners and the righteous (cf. Ps. 1.1; *Ps. Sol.* 3; *1 En.* 1.1 etc.). It is presumably this climate of thought which led our author to the bold statement: 'Nobody who remains in him sins: nobody who sins has seen or known him' (3.6); 'nobody born of God sins, because his seed (*sperma*) remains in them; such people cannot sin, because they are born of God' (3.9). The same idea is echoed towards the end of the Epistle: 'We know that nobody born (perfect participle) from God sins; but the one born (aorist participle, ? = Jesus) from God keeps them and the Evil One does not touch them' (5.18).

Every commentator wrestles with the tension—not to say downright contradiction—between these strong statements about sinlessness and the author's earlier claims that 'if we say we have no sin we deceive ourselves' (1.8), that 'if we say that we have not sinned we make him a liar' (1.10), and 'if anyone sins, we have an Advocate with the Father' (2.1). Four main approaches may be distinguished, based on: (a) Greek grammar; (b) polemical citation; (c) theological paradox; (d) rhetorical purpose.

a. *Greek Grammar*

Many have sought an explanation in the subtleties of Greek grammatical usage. The statements about the sinlessness of God's children are expressed in the present tense—'nobody who remains in him sins' (3.6, 9) etc.—whereas in 2.1, 'If anyone sins...', the verb is in the aorist. Now in ancient Greek, as in certain other languages, the different tenses may signify not only different references to time (past/present/ future) but also differences of 'aspect' or 'kinds of action'. The present stem may be used to indicate a continuous state or repeated action, while the aorist stem can indicate a momentary or 'one-off' action. So a number of scholars have suggested that what 1 John means is this: if anyone commits a particular act of sin, Jesus Christ pleads for them. But nobody born of God 'habitually' sins. Sin is not characteristic of God's children (see for example Dodd and Stott on 3.6).

But is this fine distinction what the author was really intending to express? There are several reasons for thinking that it was not. First of all, in Hellenistic Greek distinctions of 'aspect' were by no means universally observed, and one often finds present and aorist tenses side by side without distinction in meaning (e.g. Mk 1.3; Mt. 8.9). Secondly, the grammatical constructions in the two 1 John passages are not the same: in 3.6 and 3.9 the verbs that mean 'does not sin' are in the present indicative, as is appropriate for a main verb in a general statement. However, in 2.1 the verbs meaning 'sin' are not main verbs but belong to subordinate ('so that' and 'if' clauses). They are aorist subjunctives, such as are commonly used by New Testament writers in constructions of this type. The aorist was evidently preferred to the present here not for any special 'aspectual' significance it might once have carried, but because its forms had become familiar through usage. Thirdly, if the author had wanted to stress in 3.6, 3.9 and 5.18 that he was talking about *habitual sin* there are plenty of ways he could have done it more clearly. In any case 3.9 states categorically that those born from God *cannot* sin. Grammar alone is not enough to get us out of this conundrum.

b. *Polemical Citation*

H.C. Swadling has put forward an ingenious proposal: noting that *sperma* in the sense of 'divine seed' is a 'gnostic common-place', he argues that 3.6 and 3.9 are quotations from the slogans of 'gnostic' opponents (cf. also Klauck: 197-98). Since quotation marks are not shown in Greek manuscripts, this section could be paraphrased as follows (proposed slogans are italicized):

> (v. 5) You know the role of Christ to remove sins—he committed no sin at all.
> (v. 6) *Anyone who remains in him is sinless—and anyone who sins has not seen him and does not know him.*
> (vv. 7-8) Little children, let no one mislead you. It is those who act righteously who are righteous, just as Christ is righteous (etc.)...
> (v. 9) *All those who are born of God do not sin, because the divine seed remains in them; they cannot sin because they are born of God.*
> (v. 10) The way to distinguish the children of God and the children of the devil is this: those who do not act rightly are not of God, nor those who do not love their brother.

Swadling sees the author as 'demystifying' the concept of birth from divine 'seed', because opponents had claimed it brought an automatic state of sinlessness. Rather, he suggests, the reborn need to keep themselves safe (a variant reading in 5.18) and preserve themselves from habitual sin.

At a stroke, it seems, Swadling has cut the Gordian knot. But has he? There is no doubt that ancient authors did sometimes quote opponents' slogans without acknowledgment; but is this really what is happening here? The resultant sequence is jerky in thought; if recited orally a good speaker might indicate the meaning by tone of voice; in a written text one wonders whether readers could have grasped what was happening. It is ironical that the very verses which Swadling assigns to the 'opponents' are attributed by both Bogart (1979) and Brown (1982) to the author himself. They see the claims of 3.6 and 3.9 as representing 'orthodox' perfectionism, and in 1.6, 8, 10 as directed against 'heretical' perfectionism. A final problem for Swadling's view is 5.18, where he has to slip in the word 'habitual' to make his case work. If it can be supplied in 5.18, why not in 3.6 and 9? In fact, 3.4-10 hang together as a consistent unit, and vv. 7, 8 with their reference to those who 'do righteousness' (a semitism), being righteous like God, and those who 'do sin' being of the devil, far from countering 3.6 and 3.9, reinforce it. The whole passage harmonizes with our author's basic theology that righteousness and sin belong to two different 'worlds' and just do not mix.

c. *Theological Paradox*
Another approach is to explain the tension on grounds of theological paradox. It is not uncommon in biblical study to come across concepts which seem mutually incompatible: the Kingdom has arrived, but it is not yet here; 'those who are not with me are against me' (Mt. 12.30), but 'whoever is not against us is for us' (Mk 9.40); Christians are justified by faith, yet God will judge everyone according to their deeds; the believer is righteous and a sinner both at once—'simul justus et peccator' (Luther). So the tension in 1 John has been explained by the idea that the Christian as sinner lives under forgiveness, and precisely as one already sharing in salvation overcomes individual acts of sin (Braun 1951: 277). But this is a desperate playing with words. Perhaps nearer the mark is the idea that the sinlessness of those who have become God's children is an ideal, as yet imperfectly realized (so Marshall; Smalley etc.). This leads us to our final possibility.

d. *Rhetorical Purpose*
Many problems have arisen because commentators have taken 1 John too literally, without looking at its rhetorical purpose. Most people make extreme utterances occasionally in particular contexts, and it is not unusual to find logically inconsistent statements within the same political speech or

religious address. The framework of 1 John's discourse is ethical dualism. In the first part (1.5–3.3) the author sets out the need for consistency between what one claims and how one behaves, assuring readers that sins can be forgiven, but exhorting them to 'walk in the light' and not to ' love the world' (equated with darkness). They are living in the difficult last days when sin and deceit are manifest (exemplified in the antichrists)., But they are protected by the *chrisma* and the fact that they are God's children.

In his second part (3.4–5.12) he heightens his contrast between God's children who do not sin, and sinners, the children of the devil, for the destruction of whose works Jesus was manifested (3.8). In Judaism it was widely thought that in the end-time there would be no more sin among the Elect (*Ps. Sol.* 17.32; *1 En.* 5.8; *Jub.* 5.12; cf. Jer. 31.33-34). Our author sees his pupils as God's children, beloved and presumably Elect; they are living at the 'last hour' (2.11). In the eschatological conflict they are already conquerors (4.4), because the One that is with them (God) is stronger than 'the one who is in the world' (devil/antichrist). Surely they should be sinless, as befits the Elect.

Assertions like 'nobody born of God sins', though grammatically statements of fact in the indicative, serve the function of exhortation: 'Nobody born of God ought to sin' (cf. our English usage 'Nobody does that' to dissuade someone from what we believe to be wrong). In hyperbolic language the pastor seeks to promote right belief and right conduct. He does not believe that those under instruction are actually perfect; but sinlessness is what is expected of God's children; compare Deut. 18.13, 'You shall be perfect with the LORD your God'; Mt. 5.48, 'You shall be perfect as your heavenly Father is perfect' (on 'perfectionist tendencies' in Jewish and Christian literature see further Bogart 1977: ch. 4).

5. Sin unto Death?

A particularly thorny problem arises from our author's last discussion of sin, namely 5.16-17, literally: 'If anyone sees his "brother" sinning a sin not unto death, he will pray, and he [probably = God] will grant him (masc. sing.) life, to those (masc. plur.) sinning not unto death. There is a sin unto death (*hamartia pros thanaton*). I do not say that one should pray about that [sin]. Every unrighteousness is sin, and there is a sin unto death.' What is meant by this difficult passage?

It looks as if the author is following a Jewish distinction between different kinds of sin. Parts of the Hebrew Bible distinguish sharply between unconscious, inadvertent sins which could be atoned for by sacrifice (e.g. Lev. 4–7), and deliberate, wilful 'sins of a high hand', so terrible that they could never be forgiven (cf. Num. 15.30-31; Isa. 22.14; Ps. 19.13). Levitical legislation punished such sins with death, a final cutting off from the religious community (see Lev. 20.1-22; cf. Num. 18.22). At Qumran, penance was only available for those who had sinned inadvertently. Those who had deliberately sinned were permanently excluded from the community; the prescribed penances for even accidental sin were severe (1 QS 8-9; Vermes: 73-74). Other extra-biblical Jewish texts speak of certain sins leading to death, using phraseology very similar to 1 John (note esp. *T. Iss.* 7.1 [*hamartia eis thanaton*] and *Jub.* 33.13, 18). Now it is most unlikely that our author is speaking of physical death, but he may well intend a spiritual death—the opposite of 'eternal life'. One way of understanding the text would be to assume a division of sins into two classes: mortal sins (leading to eternal death) and venial or pardonable ones. It is unlikely that only accidental sin could be seen as venial, for believers all too often sin deliberately. Tertullian suggests a classification of sins into petty ones like breaking engagements and 'heavy, deadly offences' like murder, idolatry, adultery, blasphemy and denying Christ: 'for these', he says, 'Christ will no longer plead' (cited in Westcott 1902: 211). To this day the Roman Catholic Church distinguishes between venial and mortal sins on these lines. But if this is the author's meaning, he fails to make it clear. No other passage in the New Testament suggests such a distinction, which effectively limits the atoning efficacy of Jesus' death. And can one repent of a 'mortal' sin? If one can, why does the author say such a person should not be prayed for?

A more likely interpretation is that there is one particular sin which may lead to spiritual death; if a member of the community has committed this, there is no point in praying for him or her. Only one sin can fit this bill, and that is apostasy (cf. Dodd; Brooke). Apostasy—deliberate rejection of Christ once one had been converted—was viewed with the utmost seriousness in the early Church. There is reason to believe that this is the sin for which Hebrews says there is no repentance (6.4-6; 10.26). It may well be the sin against which Jesus solemnly warns in the Gospels: 'Whoever denies me before people I also will deny before my Father in heaven' (Mt. 10.32-33; cf. Lk. 9.26; 12.8-9).

Does the author think it possible that his own addressees should commit this terrible sin, or does he see it only as a possibility for his 'opponents'? It has been pointed out that 1 John speaks of seeing a *'brother'* committing a sin 'not unto death', but does not specify who might be committing a deadly sin. Scholer (1975) therefore argues that it is not possible for membership of the believing community to commit the 'sin unto death'. He suggests that it is a sin of outsiders or unbelievers—notably 1 John's opponents who had denied Christ. But he is probably reading the text too subtly. It seems more likely that 5.16-17 is a solemn warning also to the addressees that they should take care not to commit this ultimate sin. They must stand firm in their faith, obedience and love. Apostasy, that is, falling back into pagan ways in the face of persecution, was a real possibility in the early Church (cf. Edwards). So too was falling away from the right understanding of the faith. Many scholars believe that vv. 16-18 are an addition to the original text, since their teaching is not presupposed earlier. But interpreted as we have suggested, they harmonize well with 1 John's final note of warning, 'Little children, guard yourselves from "idols" [i.e. false beliefs and practices]' (5.21). One should, however, be wary of too rigid an interpretation of these disturbing verses: Origen has a wise comment: 'What kind of sins are sins to death, what not to death but to loss, cannot, I think, easily be determined by anyone' (cited in Westcott: 211).

6. Conclusion

1 John's teaching on sin and forgiveness has proved more difficult than a simple summary might suggest. It is clear that the author regards sin with the greatest abhorrence,

seeing it as incompatible with God's character and with the status of believers as God's children. In the interests of paraenesis he has articulated his concern in the sharpest possible language, using Jewish categories of thought; at the same time he affirms that sins may be forgiven through the atoning death of Jesus. The philosophical and theological problems raised by this belief lie beyond his scope.

Further Reading

In addition to the commentaries see:

J. Bogart, *Orthodox and Heretical Perfectionism in the Johannine Community* (Missoula, MT: Scholars Press, 1977).

I. Bradley, *The Power of Sacrifice* (London: Darton, Longman & Todd, 1995).

H. Braun, 'Literar-Analyse und theologische Schichtung im ersten Johannesbrief', *ZTK* 48 (1951), pp. 262-91.

E.E. Carpenter, 'Sacrifices and Offerings in the Old Testament', *ISBE* IV, pp. 260-73.

M.J. Edwards, 'Martyrdom and the *First Epistle* of John', *NovT* 31 (1989), pp. 164-71.

K. Grayston, 'The Meaning of PARAKLĒTOS', *JSNT* 13 (1981), pp. 67-82.

Lieu 1991: esp. 58-65.

S. Lyonnet and L. Sabourin, *Sin, Redemption and Sacrifice* (Rome: Biblical Institute, 1970), esp. pp. 42-45.

J.C. O'Neill, *The Puzzle of 1 John* (London: SPCK, 1966).

D.M. Scholer, 'Sins Within and Sins Without', in G.F. Hawthorne (ed.), *Current Issues in Biblical and Patristic Interpretation* (Grand Rapids: Eerdmans, 1975), pp. 230-46.

H.C. Swadling, 'Sin and Sinlessness in 1 John', *SJT* 35 (1982), pp. 205-11.

F.C. Synge, '1 John 3,2', *JTS* NS 3 (1952), p. 79.

9
CONCLUSIONS

THE INTRODUCTION TO THIS BOOK identified some key issues concerning the Johannine Epistles. Questions were raised about their composition and authorship, genre and milieu. We noted their alleged dualism, sectarianism, and polarization of attitudes, and asked how far these were consistent with their teaching on love. Problems were found with their understanding of sin. An important issue is whether these writings have any message for today. We now draw together the threads of this study and seek to assess the theological strengths and weaknesses of these intriguing writings.

1. Literary and Historical Character of the Epistles

The literary form of 2 and 3 John is that of letter. 3 John comes closest to the pattern of the simple, informal papyrus letter. It deals with specific issues—hospitality to travelling missionaries, the pretensions of a local Church leader Diotrephes, and the commendation of Demetrius (probably 3 John's bearer). 2 John seems to be a more artificial creation, probably dependent on both 3 John and 1 John. The 'elect lady' to whom it is addressed is usually interpreted as a personification of a Church, though she may be a real woman (cf. above Chapter 2 §3). Unless either *eklektē* or *kyria* is a personal name, this is the only New Testament writing to contain no proper names (other than Jesus). 2 John urges love, obedience and adherence to the truth. It also deals with the problem of 'deceivers', who may be either the same group as those denounced in 1 John, or possibly others with similar views who, the author feels, need castigation in similar language. These letters may or may not be by the same man, but they apparently come from the same Johannine 'circle' or community.

The genre of 1 John remains enigmatic. In its present form it is not a letter (whether literary or otherwise). Its general character is hortatory and paraenetic, setting out a kind of 'Two Ways' theology marked by stark antitheses (cf. the Sermon on the Mount). Like 2 and 3 John it is consciously a written document (cf. 1.4; 2.12-14; 2.26; 5.13), but at the same time it probably incorporates oral material of a catechetical kind. There is much to be said for the view that it is an *encheiridion* or handbook compiled from both oral and written sources (cf. Chapter 3 §6). It refers to deceivers, who are denounced as 'antichrists', but their identity remains obscure. There is no statement of their teachings or detailed refutation of them, but they are countered by christological challenges, for example, 'Who is the liar, but the one who denies that Jesus is the Christ?' (2.22). In spite of this material, I do not see the primary purpose of 1 John as polemical. Its main purpose is to strengthen Christian faith. Indeed, if I am right in my hypothesis that it is some kind of instruction book, references to opponents may already have lost their topical relevance, being retained out of reverence for the master's teaching or because of their wider applicability. The intended audience for 1 John is unknown. There is no mention of Gentiles or Jewish–Gentile controversies. The theological content reveals a strong debt to Judaism, and there is much to be said for the view that it was intended for a Jewish-Christian audience, probably in the Diaspora.

The relationship of 1–3 John to John's Gospel is uncertain. Similarities of language and thought suggest that they stem from the same community, though not necessarily the same author, for there are theological differences. Although some of 1 John's ideas seem more 'primitive' than the Gospel of John's (e.g. its teaching on atonement and eschatology), apparent allusions to the Gospel support the view that it was written after it. The evidence is insufficient to demonstrate that it was written specifically in *defence* of it. Stylistically

1 John has a strong Jewish and semitic flavour (there are semitisms also in 2–3 John). Its author has some natural rhetorical skill, but his Greek is marked by obscurities and ambiguities, and there are many places where his meaning is unclear. The internal evidence does not corroborate ancient traditions that the Johannines were written by the Apostle John or the shadowy 'John the Elder', known from Papias and Eusebius. But it is likely their author(s) were by origin Jewish. The basic thought-world is that of the Hebrew Bible; 1 John in particular has affinities with other Jewish writings, including the Qumran texts, *Jubilees* and the *Testaments of the Twelve Patriarchs*; it also shows some familiarity with incipient Gnosticism. However, one should not forget that 1–3 John are *Christian* writings, with many points of contact with the religious thought of other New Testament epistles and, indeed, the Gospels. The author(s) write because they are inspired by faith in Jesus Christ, as messiah, and from a sense of the love, holiness and faithfulness of God. The date of the Johannines cannot be precisely determined, but they were probably written towards the end of the first century CE.

2. Sectarianism and Dualism

We turn now to problems concerning the social and religious understanding of 1–3 John. Raymond Brown considers the question of sectarianism a 'burning issue'. He asks bluntly: 'Has the association of Johannine Christians become a sect?' (1979: 14). A number of scholars, with varying degrees of confidence or hesitancy, have answered in the affirmative, among them Meeks, Smith, Culpepper, Bogart and Segovia. Much depends on what is meant by 'sect'. In popular English usage this term is usually employed for a denomination or similar religious grouping with distinctive beliefs whose members are, of their own choice, separated from the mainstream or institutional Church. In North America 'sect' is more often used as a sociological term for an exclusive community who see themselves as separated from the surrounding society and who hold negative views of 'the world' (cf. Meeks 1972). Were the Johannine Christians a 'sect' in either of these senses?

The first point to be made is that the existence of a 'Johannine community' separated from other New Testament communities is itself a conjecture. It is true that John's Gospel and 1–3 John share a common fund of ideas emphasizing such concepts as mutual love, truth, and light–dark dualism. But the notion that these stem from a separate ecclesial community is a hypothesis, not a fact. We do not know how 'Johannine' Christians related to the Pauline Churches, the 'great Church' at Jerusalem, or other early Christian communities. For a group to be called a 'sect' in the religious sense one would expect it to have distinctive doctrines and/or distinctive forms of worship. The *Concise Oxford Dictionary* defines a sect as a 'body of persons agreed upon religious doctrines usually different from those of an established or orthodox Church from which they have separated and usually having distinctive common worship...' But we know practically nothing about the worship of Johannine Christians, not even for certain whether they practised baptism or celebrated the Lord's Supper (1–3 John say nothing about these sacraments, and John's Gospel only alludes to them indirectly). As for Church government, there is no reason to think it was very different from that found in the rest of the New Testament. Like the Pauline congregations, the Johannine churches seem to have had a 'charismatic' element with an emphasis on reception of the Spirit, accompanied by strong leadership on the part of individuals, such as Diotrephes and the Elder of 2–3 John. Although some scholars have thought the Gospel of John's portrayal of Peter implies polemic against the Petrine or 'great' Church (discussed in Quast 1989: 7-16), this is speculative, and there is no hint of such hostility in the Epistles.

Turning to religious beliefs, we must stress that the doctrinal ideas of 1–3 John (and John's Gospel) are essentially those of mainstream New Testament Christianity—the goodness and holiness of God; God's loving fatherhood and Jesus' divine sonship; human sinfulness and the need for forgiveness; the atoning death of Jesus; the gift of the Spirit; future judgment and hope of glory. The resurrection is not mentioned in 1–3 John, but Jesus' exaltation to heaven may be presupposed by his role as intercessor. 1 John does contain peculiar features, notably the terms *chrisma, sperma* and 'Antichrist', and the ideas of the impeccability (sinlessness) of God's children; also the concept of 'sin unto death'. But are these distinctive ideas more numerous or peculiar than those found uniquely in other New Testament documents (e.g. baptism for the dead in 1 Corinthians)? The ideal of eschatological sinlessness is, in any case, implied by many texts (e.g. 1 Thess. 5.23; Jude 24).

The problem with using the category of sectarianism (in the religious sense) is that it presupposes a clear-cut 'orthodoxy' or normative form of Christianity against which other manifestations of the faith can be measured. In practice, the New Testament documents exhibit a range of Christologies and soteriologies. The alternative is to regard Johannine Christianity as sectarian in contradistinction to Judaism (rather than the rest of early Christianity). If this makes it a 'sect', so too are all the other New Testament Churches.

What of the broader, more sociological understanding of 'sect', applied to inward-looking groups with 'world-denying' tendencies? The Johannine Epistles certainly presuppose a tightly-knit group who love one another, expressing their cohesiveness through such terms as 'brothers', 'beloved' and 'community' (*koinōnia*). They are hostile towards 'the world' and expect to be hated by it. They use vigorous, pejorative language for those with whom they disagree theologically, and seek to dissociate themselves from them. These features suggest a tendency towards sectarianism in the sociological sense. But are the Johannine Epistles any more 'sectarian' than other New Testament writings?

Ethical 'dualism', or a polarity between light and dark, good and evil, belief and unbelief, runs through the New Testament as a whole. Paul tells believers not to be 'mismated' with unbelievers, 'For what fellowship has light with darkness? Or what accord has Christ with Belial?' (2 Cor. 6.14). Christians are told to 'walk as children of light', taking no part in 'the unfruitful works of darkness' (Eph. 5.8, 11). They are to set their minds 'on things above, not on things on the earth' (Col. 3.2). The Epistle of James decries friendship with 'the world', holding up the ideal of keeping oneself 'unspotted' from it (1.27). Jesus himself demands a wholehearted, 'otherworldly' discipleship, bidding his followers not to lay up treasures on earth: 'no one can serve two masters... you cannot serve God and Mammon' (Mt. 6.24). In Mark 'the cares of the world and the deceit of wealth and the desires for other things' prevent the word bearing fruit (Mk 4.19). The main purpose of such ethical 'dualism' is to inculcate selfless, holy conduct. We have to face the fact that if the Johannines are 'sectarian' for expressing these views, so too is much of the rest of the New Testament.

As for attitudes to opponents, we have already commented on ancient conventions which permitted much more colourful language than is customary today. In fact, the language of the Johannines is in some respects mild compared with 2 Peter, where opponents are reviled as 'bold and wilful...like irrational animals...blots and blemishes...accursed children', for whom nether darkness has been reserved (2.10-17). In Acts, Paul castigates one opponent as 'a complete fraud and imposter, son of the devil, enemy of righteousness' (13.10); and in his letters he is not afraid to dub those with whom he differs theologically as 'pseudo-apostles and confidence tricksters' (2 Cor. 11.13). Matthew's Gospel denounces the scribes and Pharisees as hypocrites, blind guides, fools and children of Hell (Mt. 23.13-29). This does not make the Johannine attitudes any better, but it helps us understand them. Perhaps it was hoped by such language to shock people into repentance. At the very least such terms served as a warning to readers.

We conclude, then, that there is a sense in which 1–2 John are sectarian (there is not enough material to make a judgment on 3 John). But, as we have seen, they share this characteristic with many other New Testament writings. Their hyperbolic language serves to reinforce their ethical and christological purpose. It is another question whether it is right or helpful to use such language today.

3. Love and Ethical Conduct

The teaching of 1 John on love is so moving that it is hard to understand why it has come under attack in recent years. The main problems arise from a reading which presupposes that a full theology of love is being given; this is then criticized as inadequate. The teaching should be seen in its social and rhetorical context. 1 John is concerned with the fundamentals of the Christian life. The author seeks to promote love of God and mutual love among members. We can compare 1 Peter, probably also incorporating catechetical material, which sets out basics of the faith: redemption and new birth through Jesus Christ; the call to holiness and obedience, and *philadelphia*—brotherly (and sisterly) love. 'Having purified your souls in obedience to the truth so that you have genuine mutual love, *love one another* from a pure heart fervently, having been born again, not from perishable seed, but from imperishable, through the living and abiding word of God' (1 Pet. 1.22-23). Romans (12.10), 1 Thessalonians (4.9), Hebrews (13.1), and even 2 Peter (1.7) similarly urge mutual love. Some of these texts (Rom. 12.14; Heb. 13.2) also enjoin love of enemies or hospitality to strangers; but one cannot expect every Christian writing to urge every Christian duty (or touch on every Christian doctrine). 1 John is not concerned with relations with non-Christians, but with inner-Christian relationships and the believer's relationship with God.

1 John's injunction to love is rooted in its understanding of God's nature as love. The logical corollary of the great affirmation 'God is love' is that Christian love should also be universal. The author wants Christian love to be practical, including concern for both physical and spiritual needs (3.17; 5.16). He is adamant that one cannot love God without loving fellow-Christians: 'Those who say "I love God" and hate their brothers [and sisters] are liars; for how can those who do not love a brother [or sister] whom they have seen love God whom they have not seen?' (4.20). We might add, 'How can those who do not love their fellow-Christians whom they have seen love strangers whom they have not seen?' It seems to be a case of 'charity begins at home'.

Unlike many other New Testament texts, 1 John does not list rules for proper Christian conduct. There are no *Haustafeln* (tables of household rules) governing behaviour of wives and husbands, slaves and masters, such as we find in Colossians, Ephesians and 1 Peter. Though obedience to God's (or Christ's) commands is frequently enjoined, it is never spelt out what these commands are: the only one mentioned is the command to love. This is both a strength and a weakness of Johannine ethics.

4. Doctrine and Religious Experience

For some the great strength of 1 John is its championing of doctrinal orthodoxy against the threat of 'heresy'. The reality of Christ's 'coming in the flesh' is strongly upheld, and a firm stance taken against any who would deny it. Yet it is precisely this insistence on a particular understanding of Jesus' sonship and messiahship which others see as a weakness. 1 John has been characterized as 'reactionary' and 'inflexible', with its harking back to what was 'from the beginning', and sometimes contrasted adversely with the Gospel of John, which is seen as theologically 'creative'. One must reply that the Church and world need both conservative and progressive (or radical) theologians—progressive to explore and break new ground; conservative to preserve what is good. In any case 1 John is not lacking more speculative elements, for example, when it speaks of the indescribable transformation awaiting believers (3.2). Similarly, the language of 'eternal life', 'chrism', 'seed', 'having God' and 'being' or 'abiding' in God is capable of creative, mystical interpretation. This is not cut-and-dried dogmatic theology, but the language of religious experience.

One problem for modern readers is that some of the language does not correspond to their own religious experience. Some are unhappy with its androcentric language. Many are ill-at-ease with its 'black-and-white' outlook, dividing humanity into 'children of God' and 'children of the devil'. The Johannine polarization seems too sharp. What are we to make, in a modern, scientific age, of references to the 'Antichrist' and the devil? Do we take these terms literally, or do we 'demythologize' them? In a sense our author may have already started demythologizing by identifying the end-time 'Antichrist' with contemporary human beings. But one would hardly wish to imitate the medieval thinkers or Protestant Reformers who described their religious opponents (Emperors and Popes) as God's archetypal spiritual enemy. Even if 'Antichrist' is demythologized, the author still believes in an imminent *parousia*. And what about the devil? Can we believe in spiritual conflict at a cosmic level? Does the whole world lie in the power of the 'Evil One' (1 Jn 5.19)? While some Christians are content to accept this world-view, many feel that it is unduly pessimistic, that it denies the true victory of the Cross, and that it takes picture-language too literally. We no longer believe in demons as the cause of epilepsy, or mental illness or sudden disaster; we believe in our own responsibility for our actions; why bring in the devil, except as a last resort to explain the problem of evil? Even then, the hypothesis does not really account for the presence of evil in the world; for Scripture leaves unexplained how the 'devil' ('Satan', or 'the Evil One') came into being, or how a God who is all-powerful, as well as all-just and all-good, can tolerate the activities of a spiritual being which lures men and women to sin.

1 John's teaching on sin and atonement also causes difficulties for some readers. While many have found hope and encouragement in its assurances of forgiveness, especially 2.1, enshrined in the 'Comfortable Words' of the Book of Common Prayer, people are disturbed by its reference to a 'sin unto death' (5.16-17), and puzzled (or worried) by the assertion that God's children cannot sin, which runs contrary to Christian experience as well as formally contradicting what was said earlier in this writing. Some are put off by the language of 'blood' and sacrifice. How can Jesus' death remove sin? Once again we are dealing with a mode of thought alien to the modern world of computers and astrophysics. Yet here, as with the devil, 1 John's concepts are those of the rest of the Bible. He writes as heir to a long tradition of Jewish thought, in the context of other ancient faiths which made use of rituals of sacrifice and appeasement. Such concepts and rituals still have power to move and motivate (cf. Bradley 1995). Perhaps we need a radical rethinking of how Biblical ideas of sacrifice and atonement can be re-expressed in ways meaningful for a modern world. In this respect the Johannine Epistles provide stimulus for ongoing theological enquiry.

5. Conclusion

Biblical texts may serve as warnings as well as examples. Even a 'sectarian' reading of 1–3 John can teach something of the dangers of belonging to a closed group who hold to rigid doctrinal lines. At the same time we get a glimpse into the values of a community where mutual love and obedience to God's commands are taken seriously. Whatever our reading of the text, the Johannines speak to us of a God who is just and loving, and of a Saviour who gave his life for all humanity. They set before us ideals of righteousness, love and purity of conduct. They offer hope for the future and assure us of the possibility of forgiveness. However great the problems caused by their obscurity of expression or 'mythological' modes of thought, they have a message for us today. 'Trust in God's Son Jesus Christ and love one another' (1 Jn 3.23). 'Beloved, let us love one another, for love is of God' (4.7).

Further Reading

On sectarianism and relation to mainstream Christianity:
Brown 1979.
W.A. Meeks, 'The Man from Heaven in Johannine Sectarianism', *JBL* 91 (1972), pp. 44-72.
K. Quast, *Peter and the Beloved Disciple* (Sheffield: JSOT Press, 1989).
F. Segovia, 'The Love and Hatred of Jesus in Johannine Sectarianism', *CBQ* 43 (1981), pp. 258-72, esp. 258.
D.M. Smith, 'Johannine Christianity', *NTS* 21 (1975), pp. 222-48, esp. 224.

On the devil and theodicy:
Loader: 36-37.
J. Hick, *Evil and the God of Love* (London: Macmillan, 1966).

On the atonement:
D.M. Bailey, *God Was in Christ* (London: Faber & Faber, 1948), chs. 7-8 (a classic work).
I. Bradley, *The Power of Sacrifice* (London: Darton, Longman & Todd, 1995).

INDEXES

INDEX OF REFERENCES

Index of Authors